LESSER SPOTTED CLASSICS
21
GREAT CARS YOU (PROBABLY) WON'T SEE ON THE ROAD

LESSER SPOTTED CLASSICS

21

GREAT CARS YOU (PROBABLY) WON'T SEE ON THE ROAD

DAVID MILLOY

RUSSELL WALLIS

Cover, Illustrations and typeset design by
Russell Wallis
RJW|Creative Design,
www.rjwcreativedesign.co.uk
Twitter: @Russelljwallis

Printed by Amazon

To Alan and Andrew, the bravest and the best

_____

For Richard, a very generous dad

CONTENTS

INTRODUCTION

Firstly, and most importantly, please accept my thanks and those of Russell for buying this book. We hope that you enjoy it.

The cars featured in this book share a couple of things: one, they're all rare in the UK, to the point that there are a couple I've never actually seen on a UK road; and two, each and every one of them is a great car in its own way. I've owned a few of them, driven others and gazed wistfully at the ones I wanted to buy but either couldn't find or couldn't afford, sometimes both!

But why pick these particular cars? After all, surely lots of other fine cars are now on the danger list? The simple answer is that I wanted to include a varied selection of cars in the book, hence the presence of cars as dissimilar as the Jensen GT and Suzuki Cappuccino. The book would, I think, have lost something if it had just contained sports cars or British cars or cars built in a particular decade. Variety may be the spice of life, but it isn't half important in books too!

Talking of things that are important, you might be wondering where the data used in this book comes from. The statistics about the number of examples of each model that are licensed for use on UK roads or on SORN comes, with a couple of exceptions, from the DVLA, who publish publicly downloadable tables every quarter. However, you needn't download those tables and pore through the data, not when you can point your browser at www.howmanyleft.co.uk and gain quicker and more user-friendly access to it, thanks to the site's creator, Olly Smith.

The performance data given for each car has been lifted from a variety of contemporary sources. Do bear in mind, however, that no two road tests ever yield quite the same performance figures, so don't be surprised if you find data that doesn't quite agree with that which I've used. Also, please be aware that all power outputs quoted are in bhp (brake horsepower) rather than PS (pferdestärke, German for horsepower). Bhp and PS are not identical units of measurement, with 1 bhp equating to 1.014 PS. So, for example, the 210 PS of a Renault Avantime 3.0 equates to 207 bhp.

That brings me to a very important part of this introduction: the bit where I get to thank people who have in some way helped this book to become a reality rather than an idea gathering dust in the dark recesses of my mind. In no particular order, I wish to express my sincere thanks to: Bill Atkinson, Terry Webb, Simon Crosby, Dave Boneham, Phil Blake, Simon Moffat, Simon Fletcher and my partner-in-crime on the Bangers & Classics podcast (www.bangersandclassics.com), James Ruppert.

My thanks also go to Marcus T. Ward, who designed the front covers for my previous books (*The Ultimate Classic Car Quiz Book* and *The Ultimate Unofficial F1 Quiz Book*) and supplied the excellent images of F1 cars for the Kindle edition of the latter. Although Marcus wasn't able to contribute to this book because of the pressure of other work, he very kindly put me in touch with Russell.

And now I'm in the very privileged position of both knowing and having collaborated with two superb artists, both of whom I hope to work with again in the future... if they'll have me!

Russell is responsible for all of the images within the book, the covers, and its layout. I'm sure you'll agree that he's done a fantastic job. And if you're wondering why the images are in black and white, it's because of the cost of colour printing. As we wanted to offer the book at an affordable price, colour simply wasn't an option.

If you want to purchase prints of any of the images within this book then please get in touch with Russell via his website, rjwcreativedesign.co.uk, where you'll also find a terrific range of other automotive prints to buy and links to his online shops such as RJWautographics.redbubble.com. And don't forget that Marcus T. Ward also offers fantastic prints at his store: MarcusTWard. redbubble.com. As for me, please don't hesitate to get in touch via my website – just don't ask me to draw anything...

Finally, as with my previous books, a proportion (25%) of the royalties from sales of this book will go to charity. I will post monthly updates about the charities that have benefited on my website: www.thelosthighway.online.

Best wishes,

David M. Milloy

CITROËN GS BIROTOR

AT A GLANCE

Produced: 1973 to 1975
Number left in UK: Approx. 5
Engine: 995cc, twin-rotor
Power output: 106 bhp
Torque: 101 lb ft
Top speed: 109 mph
0-60 mph : 12.8 seconds

Smaller, lighter and smoother than a reciprocating engine, the rotary engine was the brainchild of Dr. Felix Wankel, who was granted a patent for a rotary engine design in 1929.

It wasn't until 1957, however, that the first running prototype rotary engines were produced: Wankel and his colleague at NSU, Hanns Dieter Paschke, each produced a running prototype that year. Paschke's design was the simpler and more practical of the two and, no doubt to Wankel's annoyance, was the one adopted for production by NSU.

Citroën was so interested in this new type of engine that they joined forces with NSU in 1964 and set up a new company, Comobil, to develop rotary engine technology. In 1967, the two companies went further, setting up Comotor, a company dedicated to the development and production of rotary engines. It would be the undoing of them both.

In 1969, Citroën produced their first rotary-engined car, the M35. A three-door coupé, the M35 was powered by a single-rotor engine and featured hydropneumatic suspension. It was not, however, intended for mass production. Rather,

Citroën planned to use the M35 as a real-world test bed by selling 500 of them to existing customers, each of whom would agree to cover at least 18,500 miles per year in their M35 and have it serviced at designated Citroën dealers, who would monitor and report on the performance of the Comotor-built engine.

The M35 was, however, expensive to buy, and this, together with Citroën's exacting requirements in terms of mileage and servicing, no doubt contributed to M35 sales falling well below the intended figure – just 267 M35s were built from 1969 to 1971. Even so, as a data-gathering exercise, the project was a success. Many of the M35s were repurchased by Citroën at the end of the test programme and subsequently scrapped, but around 90 or so have survived.

Citroën intended to follow up the M35 with three-rotor versions of its replacement for the DS, scheduled for launch in 1974. First, though, came a twin-rotor version of the GS, known as the Birotor.

Launched in 1973, the Birotor shared relatively few components with other members of the GS range – its engine, gearbox (a three-speed semi-automatic), floorpan, wheels, brakes, suspension, interior trim and many of the exterior panels differed from those found on other GS models.

The Birotor's engine produced 106 bhp but was a little lacking in low-end torque, a characteristic of rotary engines. It could have done with an extra gear ratio as well but it was still the quickest GS by some margin, having a top speed of just shy of 110 mph and being able to reach 60 mph from a standing start in just under 13 seconds.

The Birotor rode well, had better handling and grip than its lesser siblings, and its plusher trim gave it a more upmarket feel, as befitted a model that cost about 70% more than the next most expensive GS. Its price meant, however, that it was never likely to be more than a niche model.

It wasn't just expensive to buy. Rotary engines were renowned for their poor fuel economy, and the Birotor's engine was no exception, on average drinking a gallon of petrol for every 18 miles covered. It was the thirstiest car in the entire Citroën range.

In normal times, it would probably have been fair to say that if you could afford to buy a Birotor then you could afford to keep its fuel tank topped up. The Birotor was not, however, born in normal times. Instead, it had the misfortune to be launched in the same month that the Yom Kippur War broke out in the Middle East. The conflict was still raging when the Organization of Arab Petroleum Exporting Countries imposed an oil embargo targeted at countries whom they perceived to be supporting Israel. Although France was not one of those countries, it was nonetheless affected by the massive rise in fuel prices that resulted from the embargo. It was hardly the ideal time in which to try to sell a car with poor fuel consumption.

Birotor sales were further depressed by the reputation that rotary engines had gained for unreliability. This largely stemmed from the debacle surrounding the NSU Ro80, the engine of which was almost identical to that of the Birotor.

The Ro80 had caused quite a stir when launched in 1967 due to its twin-rotor engine and clean, futuristic lines. So much so that it was awarded the title of European Car of the Year for 1968. But then the problems started. The Ro80's engine suffered from excessive wear of its rotor tip seals, which led to expensive warranty claims. Public confidence in the Ro80 was badly affected and this was reflected in its sales figures.

Having invested heavily in Comotor, and with its flagship product draining its finances, NSU merged with (for which read: 'was taken over by') Volkswagen in 1969. Under VW ownership, the Ro80 continued to be built, but its reputation had been so sullied, however, that just 37,398 were built during its decade-long production run.

The cloud that covered the Ro80 also hovered over the Birotor. It didn't matter that the Comotor engine fitted to the Birotor had been improved as a result of lessons learned from the Ro80, it was tarred with the same brush. Not good, but worse was to follow.

Having bet the house on rotary engines and spent heavily on the development of the GS and CX models, Citroën found itself in dire financial straits by 1974. At the request of the French government, Peugeot invested in its ailing compatriot, taking a 38.2% stake in December 1974 and increasing it to 89.5% in 1976.

Cost-cutting and rationalisation quickly became the orders of the day under Peugeot's ownership. Given its poor sales, (unfairly) tarnished reputation,

appetite for fuel, and relative lack of shared components with other models, the Birotor was a prime candidate for the axe. And so it proved, with production being halted after just 847 cars had left the factory. As manufacturing and stocking spare parts for such a low-volume model was not financially prudent, Citroën offered generous terms to buy back every Birotor that had found a home. The cars that were repurchased were then scrapped along with every example still on the production line and the entire stock of parts.

Birotor owners who had chosen to reject Citroën's offer were on their own.

It's not known precisely how many Birotors remain in existence, but a figure of 200 may not be too far from the mark. There are perhaps four or five Birotors in the UK, of which at least two are roadworthy.

There's much to admire about the Birotor. It's an attractive, comfortable, and technologically very interesting car. And with so few having survived, the only people more fortunate than those who see a Birotor on the road are those who own one.

BMW Z1

AT A GLANCE

Produced: 1989 to 1991
Number left in UK: 52 on the road, 64 on SORN
Engine: 2494cc, six cylinder in-line, SOHC
Power output: 168 bhp
Torque: 164 lb ft
Top speed: 134 mph
0-60 mph : 7.9 seconds

Every now and then car manufacturers do something surprising – such as Lotus producing a car with front-wheel drive, Lamborghini building a V12-powered 4x4 SUV in the 1980s, and BMW creating a roadster without conventional doors, the wonderfully idiosyncratic Z1.

The Z1 (the 'Z' stands for 'Zukunft', the German word for 'future') was the first brainchild of BMW Technik, a division of the company which had been created in 1985 and was charged with developing new ideas, vehicles and technologies. The following year, a BMW press statement announced that "BMW Technik AG has completed its first product. The BMW Z1, a vehicle study, was conceived on the basis of specifications which build on longstanding BMW traditions at the same time as factoring in future mobility requirements."

What the press release didn't say was that the Z1 had already passed beyond the stage of being merely a vehicle study and was destined to go into production.

The physical fruits of Technik's creativity broke cover at the 1987 Frankfurt Motor Show, attracting considerable attention for a number of reasons. First off, the Z1 was a two-seat roadster, and BMW

hadn't produced one of those since the 1950s. Secondly, its external body panels were made from plastic. Three different grades of plastic were used, each having different levels of thickness and elasticity. This latter feature necessitated the use of a different paint lacquer for each grade of plastic but the base coat remained the same. In addition to being able to absorb minor impacts, the Z1's panels could, said BMW, be removed in about 45 minutes. Moreover, as they were not load-bearing, the Z1 could be driven with the body panels removed.

The Z1's chassis was composed of a hot-dip galvanised steel tub, which offered protection against corrosion as well as adding strength and rigidity. Its floorpan was made of composite materials (two layers of GRP-reinforced epoxy resin sandwiching a polyurethane foam centre) and was strong, light, and like the body panels, would never rust.

And then there were the doors. There weren't any. Well, not in the conventional sense: the Z1's doors could be retracted into the sills to allow access and egress. In some countries, the UK included, the Z1 could legally be driven with its doors in the 'down' position. The doors could be decried as a gimmick but the high sills their design necessitated not only added strength but enabled stylist Harm Lagaay to give the Z1 an elegantly simple yet forward-looking appearance.

The Z1 was designed with an emphasis on safety, hence a roll-over bar was housed within the windscreen header and A-pillars. Further accident protection came in the form of those high sills and a transverse tubular steel brace behind the dashboard. Dynamic safety was part of the equation too, with disc brakes all round and an anti-lock braking system (still a bit of a novelty in the early 90s) as standard.

The Z1's engine was the same 2494cc SOHC straight-six unit fitted to the contemporary 325i but mounted ten inches further back in the Z1. Noted for its smoothness, it produced 168 bhp and 164 lb ft of torque and was paired with a five-speed manual transmission.

The front suspension was also lifted from the 325i but the rear suspension was new: a multi-link axle with two transverse and one longitudinal control arms. BMW named its new rear suspension after the car, and the term 'Z-axle' thus entered the

automotive lexicon. Steering was by means of a power assisted rack and pinion set up, and the Z1 sat on seven-spoke alloy wheels shod with wide, low profile 225/45 tyres as befitted a car aimed at enthusiastic drivers.

Barring some minor switchgear, the Z1's interior was unique too. As with all BMWs of its time, the instruments (smaller than in other BMWs), pedals, and gearlever were positioned with the needs of the driver in mind. The seats, unique to the Z1, looked a little like slightly more avant-garde Renault '*Petale*' seats that had been to a health farm, and as such were very much in harmony with the Z1's looks and technocentric vibe. Protection from the elements came in the form of a manually operated fabric hood, which came as a bit of a let down in comparison to the doors.

Although limited production commenced in 1988, it was March 1989 before Z1s started to leave the production line in appreciable numbers. As it arrived a little before the great financial crash of 1990, it was initially in great demand even at an asking price of 83,000 Deutschmarks. Indeed, such was the demand for the Z1 in its early days on sale that some sharp individuals made a tidy profit by either selling their Z1 or their place in the order book for a premium – a trick we've recently seen repeated with the Toyota Yaris GR. Some things never change.

When you finally got your hands on a Z1, you'd find yourself driving it from the left-hand seat: it was never offered in right-hand drive. You'd also discover that it was tricky to get into and out of, had a very compact cabin, a tiny boot, and wasn't outrageously quick – 0 to 60 mph took 7.9 seconds and it ran out of steam (on autobahns and test tracks, of course) at 134 mph. Oh, and if you chose to remove its body panels (perhaps to replace them with ones of a different colour), you'd find that BMW's claim that they could be removed in 45 minutes was more founded in hope than reality. On the other hand, you'd undoubtedly be delighted to find that the Z1's handling and roadholding were exceptional, particularly in the dry, a feat made possible by its near-perfect weight distribution and sophisticated rear suspension.

A fine car, then, but one that was gone all too soon. Demand fell after the initial clamour subsided, no doubt at least partly as a consequence of a somewhat straitened economy, and production ended in the middle of 1991. All told, 8012 Z1s were built, a figure that includes 66 examples given the Alpina treatment and sold as the Alpina RLE. There was no direct replacement for the Z1. Indeed, when the next BMW 'Z' car, the Z3, came along five years later, it was in the form of a conventional roadster with none of the Z1's innovative features. Indeed, unlike some other BMWs of the era (and, for that matter, the Rover 75), it even lacked the Z1's innovative rear suspension set up.

Although the Z1 isn't a common sight on UK roads, your chances of seeing one are rising. Indeed, with 52 on the road as at the third quarter of 2020 and a further 62 on SORN, there are more Z1s in the UK today than there were in 1994.

Perhaps that shouldn't be a surprise, though. After all, the Z1 has always been a little different. And what's more it still looks great, it's still gloriously idiosyncratic, and it's still expensive to buy. I repeat: some things never change.

FORD ESCORT RS 1600i

AT A GLANCE
Produced: 1981 to 1983
Number left in UK: 77 on the road, 364 on SORN
Engine: 1597cc, four cylinder in-line, SOHC
Power output: 115 bhp
Torque: 109 lb ft
Top speed: 116 mph
0-60 mph : 8.7 seconds

The 1980s is remembered for many things: royal weddings, video games, the advent of the Compact Disc, glossy American soap operas, the 1987 stock market crash, the thawing of the Cold War, the Space Shuttle, E.T., the Sony Walkman, and Diego Maradona.

It is also renowned as being the golden age of the hot hatchback, a time when just about every manufacturer who sold mainstream cars in Europe offered at least one warmed-up family hatchback in its model range.

Such cars were, however, still relatively few in number when Ford made its debut in the sector with the 1980 launch of the Escort XR3. Offered only in three-door form, the XR3 was equipped with a 1.6 litre version of Ford's new CVH engine fed by a twin-choke Weber carburettor, and mated in early examples to a four-speed manual gearbox. However, its main rival, the Volkswagen Golf GTI, was able to boast of having both Bosch K-Jetronic fuel injection and a five-speed gearbox. Moreover, the Golf had more power (110 bhp against 96 bhp), torque (103 lb ft versus 96 lb ft), and was 25 kilogrammes lighter than the Ford. Even so, the XR3 with its shorter final drive ratio was able to give the

Golf GTI a run for its money in terms of straightline performance. It also at least matched the VW in terms of grip and handling but was let down by its atrocious ride quality.

The pace of hot hatch development was rapid in the 1980s, and the fitment of a 1.8 litre engine to the Golf GTI in 1982 gave it a clear performance advantage over the XR3. Meanwhile, Ford had not one but two teams working on cars based on the XR3. The resultant cars – the RS1600i and the XR3i – featured similar, though not identical, specifications, competed for the same customers, and went on sale within a few months of each other. Two obvious questions arise: why did Ford choose to release two hot hatch versions of the same car at almost the same time, and what were the differences between them?

The first question is by far the quicker to answer: the XR3i and the RS1600i were created in two countries with different objectives in mind. In the UK, Ford's Special Vehicle Engineering group was busy addressing the XR3's bone-shaking ride and equipping it with a more powerful fuel injected version of the CVH engine in order to take the fight to the Golf GTI on the sales front. At the same time, Ford's Motorsport and Rallye Sport divisions in Germany were also working on an XR3-based Escort, with the principal intention of homologating it for Group A motorsport. The result was the first-ever front-wheel drive Ford to wear an RS badge: the RS 1600i.

When the XR3i and RS 1600i reached the UK market in 1982, they shared the same three-door shell, interior architecture and Bosch K-jetronic fuel injection system. Their 1.6 litre CVH engines were similar too, but the RS1600i had a somewhat wilder camshaft profile which gave it an additional 10 bhp over the 105 bhp offered by the XR3i. There was, however, a price to pay for this extra power: the RS1600i's power delivery was rather more peaky than that of the XR3i. Indeed, it only had an edge over its stablemate at higher engine speeds, and even then some of that extra urge went to waste due to the RS1600i being limited to a maximum engine speed of 6500 rpm.

The two cars shared the same front brakes, but whereas the RS1600i was equipped with the same 7 inch diameter rear drums as the XR3, the XR3i had larger, 8 inch rear drums. The suspension set ups also differed, with the XR3i being equipped with revised front struts, which eliminated positive camber on the front wheels, as well as a thicker anti-roll bar and conventional rear coil springs rather than the dual rate springs fitted to the XR3. The RS1600i lacked the revised front struts but nonetheless featured a number of improvements over the XR3, including the fitment of additional front compression struts, a separate transverse mounting for the front anti-roll bar, lower spring platforms (the RS1600i rode almost an inch – 2.7 cm – lower than the XR3i) and Koni adjustable dampers.

There were cosmetic differences too, with the RS1600i's specification including 15 inch seven-spoke alloy wheels as standard as well as a black front air dam with driving lights, a redesigned twin-slot rear spoiler, the removal of the 'spats' at the rear of the front, and the front of the rear, wheelarches, and striping to the bonnet and flanks. On the other hand, XR3i customers had to fork out an additional £125 over the basic price if alloys (attractive 14 inch teledial-style wheels) were desired. The interiors of both were plusher than that of the XR3, with the RS1600i having a suitably sporty feel thanks to its supportive bucket-style front seats and larger diameter steering wheel.

The RS1600i's extra bells and whistles came at a premium, however, with it costing £6700 in 1983 compared to the £6030 asked for an XR3i with steel wheels.

On the road, both the RS1600i and XR3i were an improvement over the XR3. Given its higher price and extra horsepower, you would be forgiven for thinking that the RS1600i was the more accomplished of the two. In reality, however, there was little to choose between it and the XR3i. The RS1600i felt the livelier of the pair but it was no faster than the XR3i in a straight line. They were also very evenly matched in terms of grip and handling, with the sportier feel of the RS1600i being matched by the XR3i's better ride quality. Each of the two was good enough to offer stiff competition to the Golf GTI, but it's difficult not to think that Ford missed the opportunity to create something really special by making a model that combined the best features of the RS1600i and XR3i.

As a series production car, the XR3i was built in considerably greater numbers than the RS1600i, of which Ford was obliged to build 5000 examples for homologation in Group A. In the event, 8659 examples of the RS 1600i were made, of which 2608 found homes in the UK. Of that number, 77 remain on the road according to the most recent figures from the DVLA, with another 376 on SORN.

Good, and sometimes exceptional, examples of the RS1600i come up for sale fairly often. And as was the case back in their heyday, the RS1600i tends to command a slightly higher price than an XR3i in similar condition. That said, which is the better of the two remains a matter of debate. As Mark Twain once wrote: "You pays your money and you takes your choice."

LANCIA MONTECARLO

AT A GLANCE

Produced: 1976 to 1978, 1980 to 1981
Number left in UK: 67 on the road, 131 on SORN
Engine: 1995cc, four cylinder in-line, DOHC
Power output: 120 bhp
Torque: 121 lb ft
Top speed: 118 mph
0-60 mph : 8.6 seconds

The Montecarlo started out life in the late 1960s as a design sketch for a new mid-engined Fiat. Originally known as the X1/8, it was re-designated X1/20 in 1972.

Although the first prototype appeared as early as 1970, it wasn't until the 1975 Geneva Motor Show that it was first shown in production form, but as the Lancia Beta Montecarlo rather than the Fiat X1/20.

Series production was slated to begin in at Pininfarina's Grugliasco factory in early 1976. However, that forecast turned out to be a little optimistic. Two models were offered: the Coupé, with a conventional steel roof, and the Spider, essentially a 'targa' version with a fabric roof that folded into a recess between the B-pillars. Both models shared the same virtues of striking (if a little chunky to some eyes) Pininfarina-penned lines, a comfortable (albeit less so for tall drivers) and well-finished interior, and a respectable amount of luggage space.

The Montecarlo went well too: its mid-mounted 2.0 litre DOHC engine delivered a good compromise between performance and fuel economy, the latter being very important in the inflationary 1970s. Ride, handling and roadholding were also impressive, with little body roll and a tendency to understeer unless provoked.

On the negative side, the solid rear three-quarter buttresses of early Montecarlos impaired rear visibility, engine noise was poorly suppressed, and the brakes had a serious flaw. Although the Montecarlo was equipped with disc brakes all round, only the front brakes had servo assistance. Too much servo assistance, as it happened. The result was that the front wheels had an unpleasant tendency to lock under hard braking, particularly on wet or damp surfaces.

For the US market, the Montecarlo was available in Spider form only, had a different name ('Scorpion'), a smaller (1756cc), less powerful engine, higher ride height, ungainly impact-absorbing bumpers, and round headlamps that looked flush but raised a few inches when in use.

Lancia had to rename the Montecarlo for the US market as Chevrolet already produced a 'Monte Carlo' coupé. The other changes from the Montecarlo could all be put down to one thing: legislation. None of them did the Scorpion any favours. Most damning of all was the substitution of a 1.8 litre engine developing 81 bhp for the 120 bhp 2.0 litre engine fitted to the Montecarlo. The loss of 39 bhp was bad enough, but the Scorpion was also around 82 kilogrammes (180 pounds) heavier than the Montecarlo. The effect on its performance was disastrous: with a 0 to 60 mph time of 13.4 seconds, there was no sting in this Scorpion's tail. For a car that looked like a supercar, bumpers notwithstanding, the Scorpion's lack of power and pace damned it to failure. As renowned US car magazine *Road & Track* observed, the Scorpion was "so lovely, so agile, so ingenious, so slow..." Even an appearance as Herbie's, er, love interest in the 1977 Disney film *Herbie Goes To Monte Carlo* couldn't boost sales sufficiently to prevent Lancia from withdrawing the Scorpion from sale in 1977 after only 1805 had been built.

The Montecarlo was withdrawn from sale too, albeit the primary reason for its departure from the market in 1978 was the aforementioned problems with the brakes. It was an issue that should have been – and was – easy to fix, but the Montecarlo disappeared from sale for nearly two years, returning in 1980 with larger brake discs and calipers and without servo assistance. There were a few other alterations such as a new grille and larger (14 inch rather than 13 inch) but less attractive wheels. Its name had also changed: it was now known simply as the Lancia Montecarlo, a change many people felt was for the, ahem, Beta.

The Montecarlo's return to the market was, however, short-lived. Production ended in 1981, although 'new' examples continued to be sold until 1983.

As the last Montecarlos to leave the showroom were being driven home by their new owners, the Lancia 037 Group B rally car, the centre section of which came from the Montecarlo, was en route to becoming the last two-wheel drive car to win the World Rally Championship. That victory came almost a decade after another car with close links to the Montecarlo – the Abarth SE-030 Pininfarina – competed in the 1974 Giro Automobilistico d'Italia. Two of these Fiat X1/20-based, V6-powered competition cars, with distinctive 'periscope' air intakes, were built, but only one of them took part in the Giro. It showed well, finishing second to a 'works' Lancia Stratos

Turbo, but the project was thereafter shelved.

The Montecarlo's racing career didn't end, however, with the cessation of the Abarth 030 project, for in 1979 a Group 5 version of the Montecarlo took to the track to compete in the under 2000cc category of the World Championship for Makes. The Group 5 Montecarlo was a 'silhouette' racer; like the 037, it shared only its centre section with the roadgoing Montecarlo. Powered by small (1.4 litre and, later, 1.7 litre) turbocharged engines, the Group 5 Montecarlo was hugely successful, winning the under 2000cc category of the World Championship for Makes in 1979 and the overall championship in both 1980 and 1981, the latter being run under a new name: the World Endurance Championship of Makes.

In all, just 7578 Montecarlos and Scorpions were built, to which can be added 220 roadholding ('Stradale') versions of the Lancia 037. The Montecarlo was built in RHD form and around 1000 were imported to the UK, of which fewer than 200 are now known to the DVLA. In addition, there's at least one Lancia Scorpion in the UK plus a small number of 037 Stradales.

You'll be fortunate indeed to spot a Montecarlo on UK roads but if you see a Scorpion or 037 then you might want to buy a Euromillions ticket while your luck's in.

MG MAESTRO TURBO

AT A GLANCE

Produced: 1989
Number left in UK: 21 on the road, 161 on SORN
Engine: 1994cc, four cylinder in-line, turbocharged, SOHC
Power output: 152 bhp
Torque: 169 lb ft
Top speed: 131 mph
0-60 mph : 6.6 seconds

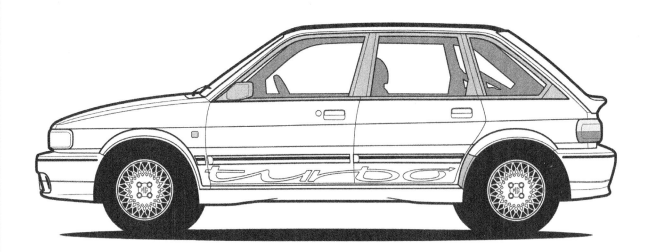

In its original guise, the Austin Maestro was, at best, the sort of worthy, uninspiring car that was destined to be forever damned by faint praise.

It was roomy enough, drove adequately well, and its four doors plus hatchback configuration gave it a useful degree of versatility. Indeed, in just about every respect the Maestro was a big improvement over its predecessor, the Morris Ital.

On the other hand, its styling looked dated even at launch, it lacked the sort of quality and innovation that was needed to make an impact in a very competitive market sector, and its build quality was patchy at best. If ever a car needed to have an image boost, the Maestro was it.

A halo model was the obvious answer. Step forward the MG Maestro.

At launch in 1983, the Maestro range included a warmed-up version that, controversially to some, wore an MG badge. This car, the MG Maestro, was powered by a twin-carb version of the 1.6 litre 'R' series engine that powered more sedate members of the Maestro range.

The decision to include a sporty model in the Maestro range was made late in the model's development. Austin Rover had noted the success of the 'hot' versions of two of the Maestro's key rivals, the VW Golf and Ford Escort, and had determined that they needed to follow suit. Unfortunately, this meant that the MG Maestro was undeveloped in its original guise, a consequence of which was that it suffered from hot starting and fuel vaporisation problems. This was less of a problem on cool days and on open roads with plenty of airflow, but hot days and heavy traffic could result in a very frustrated driver.

In terms of pace, it wasn't quite a match for its VW and Ford rivals and its chassis was a little lacking in composure. Its interior was livened up by the use of red carpets and red seat belts, and there was an electronic instrument panel and a driver information system that conveyed messages via a speech synthesizer – an idea that worked better in theory than in practice.

The impact of the MG's exterior enhancements – red MG badging, red piping to the bumpers and side impact strips, and attractive alloy wheels that were a pain to clean – was dulled by its frumpy shape. Simply put, it just didn't have the sort of looks that would appeal to its target market.

There wasn't much that BL could do about that,

but they could improve the MG Maestro in other ways. Their first move was to replace the 'R' series engine with an 'S' series unit, but a more significant step was taken in the second half of 1984 with the launch of the new MG Maestro EFI. With power supplied by a by a fuel-injected, 2.0 litre version of the 'O' series engine, its performance (115 mph, 0 to 60 in 8.7 seconds) was a match for its main rivals.

The suspension received some welcome upgrades too. A rear anti-roll bar was fitted (a curious omission from the 1.6 litre version), a thicker front anti-roll bar was specified, and the front dampers were uprated. The steering was a little over-sensitive but handling, grip, and ride quality were all good. The brakes were mostly left untouched, save for the fitment of ventilated rather than solid front discs.

In this new guise, the MG Maestro became the car it should have been from the start. It was neither the fastest nor the sharpest of hot hatchbacks but it was a competent performer across the board. A good car, then, but one that wasn't thereafter developed in response to the strides made by its competitors. In the two years following the launch of the MG Maestro EFI, Ford brought out the

Escort RS Turbo, VW produced a 16V version of the Golf GTI, Peugeot introduced the 1.9 litre version of the 205 GTI, and Vauxhall, Renault, Lancia, and Fiat all introduced uprated versions of previous models. Competition for sales in the hot hatchback sector was fierce, and the customer was the winner.

Consideration had been given to producing a turbocharged MG Maestro in 1984 but the idea did not gain universal approval, with Austin Rover's chairman, Harold Musgrove, revealing at the time that he was one of those who was against it.

But whilst the MG Maestro soldiered on in normally aspirated form, an MG Turbo version of its booted cousin, the Montego, was introduced in 1985. Using a turbocharged version of the 2.0 litre 'O' series engine, the MG Montego Turbo could hit 60 mph from standstill in 7.4 seconds on its way to a top speed of 129 mph. It was enough to turn MG Maestro owners green with envy.

It took a couple of years, the departure of Harold Musgrove, and the arrival of ever more powerful rivals before work started on a blown version of the MG Maestro. And when it did arrive, complete with the 2.0 litre turbocharged unit from the MG Montego Turbo, it was 1989, Austin Rover Group had become Rover Group plc, and British Aerospace plc was its majority shareholder.

Assembly of each MG Maestro Turbo (officially it was known as the Maestro MG Turbo but we'll stick with its more commonly used name) began at Rover's Cowley production plant, after which they were shipped to Tickford's facility at Bedworth to have their body kits and decals added. They then made the return trip to Cowley before being dispatched to dealers.

With 152 bhp and 169 1b ft of torque on tap, the MG Maestro Turbo could sprint from 0 to 60 mph in a class-leading time of 6.6 seconds and go on to a top speed of 131 mph. Its appearance was toughened up too, courtesy of a Tickford produced body kit with integrated front driving lamps. Equipment levels were good, with electric front windows, central locking, alloy wheels, and a sunroof all fitted as standard, and it had a roomy, well-finished cabin.

As a package, however, it fell short of the best of its competitors, for although it had ample grip its ride was overly firm and its nose-heavy (66/34) weight distribution meant that its handling was somewhat lacking in finesse – it was a bludgeon rather than a rapier. And as you'd expect, the Turbo was somewhat more thirsty than its less powerful rivals.

Rover had in mind from the start to limit production of the MG Maestro Turbo to 500 examples but were coy about announcing this lest demand justify an extended production run. As it turned out, they needn't have worried about extending the production run: sales were on the sluggish side of steady, and dealers were still offering 'new' examples over a year after production ended in November 1989. In all, 505 MG Maestro Turbos were built, with Flame Red being the most popular of the four colours (red, green, black, and white) in which it was offered.

The normally aspirated MG Maestro, latterly sold as the MG Maestro 2.0i, lasted a little longer and sold in appreciably higher numbers. However, none of the MG-badged Maestros now exist in large numbers: just seven of the 1.6 litre cars, 37 of the 2.0 litre and 21 of the Turbos were licensed with the DVLA as at the third quarter of 2020.

With so few around, you'll be lucky to catch one ...if you can.

BOND BUG

AT A GLANCE

Produced: 1970 to 1974
Number left in UK: 157 on the road, 118 on SORN
Engine: 701cc, four cylinder in-line, OHV
Power output: 31 bhp
Torque: 38 lb ft
Top speed: 76 mph
0-60 mph : 23.7 seconds
(Performance figures for 700ES model)

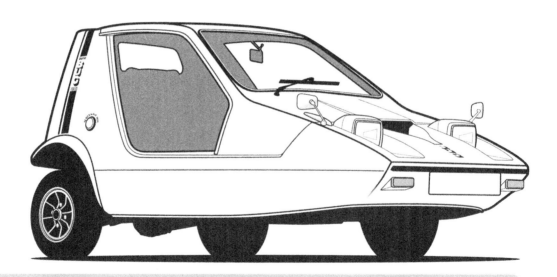

Oddly enough, the most famous Bond of them them all, barring a certain fictional spy, wasn't really a Bond at all but a badge-engineered Reliant: the Bond Bug.

The Bug's roots lay in a 1963 design by Tom Karen of Ogle Design for a three-wheel sports car. Reliant was then one of Ogle's clients, and Karen hoped that his proposal for a sporty three-wheeler might find favour with them. It didn't.

By 1968, however, Reliant's views had changed somewhat. Perceiving that there was now a market for a fun, youth-oriented car, they commissioned Tom Karen to revisit his earlier proposal. The result was the creation of a full-size prototype, the Reliant Rogue. It would almost certainly have gone into production under that name but for Reliant's purchase of Bond Cars Ltd., a fellow manufacturer of low-volume three- and four-wheel cars, in early 1969.

Reliant was keen to introduce a new Bond, and so the Reliant Rogue became a Bond. It acquired a new name too, Tom Karen having suggested that it be called the Bug.

Meantime, Karen had been hard at work on his design for the Rogue. Reliant liked the Rogue prototype but felt that it needed some changes (the addition of some boot space and a wider front end) in order to be viable as a production car. Karen duly made these changes, and thus emerged the unmistakable shape of the Bond Bug.

Launched in 1970 at Woburn Abbey, the Bug caused quite a stir with its vivid tangerine paintwork, wedge shape, front-hinged canopy (it had no doors), bug-eyed lights, and exposed rear axle. Built on a newly designed chassis (that would later be used on the Reliant Robin), it was powered by Reliant's 701cc OHV engine and offered in two states of tune.

There were three models offered at launch: the basic 700 (of which only one example was ever built), the higher-spec 700E, and the top-of-the-range 700ES, which featured a higher compression version of the 701cc pushrod engine.

The Bug's front-mounted engine drove the rear wheels via a four-speed manual gearbox, which lacked synchromesh on first gear. In its higher-compression form, the engine produced 31 bhp and 38 lb ft of torque, enough to propel the Bug to a top speed of 76 mph and from rest to 60 mph in a smidgeon under 24 seconds. To put those figures into context, a Mini 850 ran out of steam at 70 mph and took four seconds longer to cover the 0 to 60 sprint.

The Bug was ideally suited to city traffic. Its size (it was a mere 2.8 metres long) and weight, allied to direct steering (2.2. turns lock to lock) gave it excellent manoeuvrability and the ability to fit into small parking spaces. Its good handling, roadholding, and stability (particularly with two occupants) meant that it coped well with the open road too, although its ride was somewhat jiggly on rougher surfaces.

As per Tom Karen's suggestion, the Bug was only ever offered in one colour: tangerine. A few were, however, produced in both lime green and white for companies intending to use them for promotional purposes.

The bodyshells of early Bugs were produced at Bond's factory in Preston and thereafter shipped to Reliant's factory at Tamworth to be united with the chassis and running gear. That arrangement came to an end after just a few months, when Bug production was transferred to Tamworth ahead of the closure of the Bond factory.

In October 1973, the Bug received Reliant's 748cc engine as standard. The range now consisted of the 750E and the 750ES. By then, however, the writing was on the wall for the Bug. Sales had been disappointing and production had slowed, and only 142 of the 748cc models were built between their introduction in October 1973 and the end of Bug production the following May. But that wasn't the end of the road for the Bug.

Reliant had experimented with a four-wheel Bug, and at least one prototype was built by them in 1970. Although they chose not to proceed with the idea, it would come to fruition two decades later, when Bug enthusiasts Michael and Gary Webster acquired not only the Bug moulds but the right to use the Bug name.

The result was that the Webster Motor Company ('WMC') offered both four-wheel and three-wheel Bugs in kit form, the former of which used a modified version of the Bug's ladder-type chassis mated to the front subframe from a Mini. As a result, the wheelbase of the four-wheel WMC Bug was around 20cm longer than that of the original. WMC is believed to have sold around twenty to thirty of the four-wheel Bug kits and four of the three-wheeler kits.

In 1995, Reliant decided to put an updated version of the Bug into production. An agreement was reached with the Websters which resulted in certain intellectual property rights returning to Reliant, the Bug's original designer, Tom Karen, produced an updated body design, and a prototype was built. The Bug name was not revived, however, and the new model would instead be known as the Reliant Sprint.

The Sprint was scheduled for launch in 1996, but before that could happen Reliant went into administration. A buyer was found but the Sprint project was abandoned in favour of a plan to put a new four-wheel 'Bug' into production in both coupé and open-top form. As with the Sprint before it, the project was halted after a prototype was built. This four-wheel 'Bug', the styling of which took its cues from the Sprint, still exists and can be seen at the Bubble Car Museum in Boston, Lincolnshire.

Reliant finally ceased to manufacture cars in 2002.

Including the original Reliant four-wheel prototype from 1970 but excluding the WMC cars and later prototypes, 2270 Bond Bugs were built.

Five decades on from its launch, there's still nothing quite like a Bond Bug, both in terms of its looks and its extraordinary ability to make people smile. The good news is that your chances of seeing one have been improving year on year for a considerable time. According to the DVLA, 157 Bugs were licensed in the UK as at the third quarter of 2020, with another 118 on SORN. By way of comparison, 97 Bugs were on the road and 64 on SORN in 2007.

The reason for this increase is simple: many Bugs that were no longer roadworthy were tucked away in garages, workshops, and barns rather than carted off to the scrapyard. And now that values are rising (a restored Bug sold for over £29,000 at auction in February 2021), some of those hidden Bugs have emerged from their lairs and been re-registered. Long may it continue.

CHRYSLER /TALBOT SUNBEAM Ti

AT A GLANCE

Produced: 1979 to 1981
Number left in UK: 6 on the road, 83 on SORN
Engine: 1598cc, four cylinder in-line, OHV
Power output: 100 bhp
Torque: 96 lb ft
Top speed: 105 mph
0-60 mph : 10.3 seconds

In the 1960s, Chrysler dreamed of emulating Ford and General Motors, its fellow members of the 'Big Three' US car producers, by adding a substantial European enterprise to its Stateside operations. But rather than build up the Pentastar brand from scratch in Europe, Chrysler elected to purchase established car manufacturers on both sides of the English Channel: Simca in France, Rootes in the United Kingdom.*

It was an astute move on the face of it, but it turned out to be a disaster, largely due to Chrysler's failure to integrate its European manufacturing arms.

Simca, in which Chrysler obtained a controlling interest in 1963, had considerable success in the 1960s with its boxy, rear-engined 1000 saloon and, from 1967, with its advanced 1100 range. The latter, a hit with both critics and consumers, joined the Renault 16 in pointing the way forward for European car design, having front-wheel drive, all-round independent suspension, and a hatchback configuration.

Rootes, on the other hand, was a rather more conservative company in terms of design and engineering. With the exception of the Imp and its derivatives, the Rootes range was composed of conventionally styled saloons and estate cars, with front-mounted engines that drove the rear wheels. For the most part, its cars were worthy but staid, and car buyers were increasingly looking for something more than that.

The Imp might have been the car to help Rootes break free of its sedate image but issues with industrial relations, quality control, and reliability, in addition to fierce competition in the form of the Mini, meant that it never sold in anything like the numbers that its makers had hoped.

Chrysler therefore found itself in control of two car manufacturers with different philosophies and incompatible mechanical components. The obvious solution was to rationalise their running gear and harmonise their efforts. Unfortunately, that never happened.

In 1970, Chrysler UK launched the Avenger, a range of small family saloons and estate cars in the manner of Ford's highly successful Escort. The Avenger, which stuck to the front-engine, rear-drive recipe, was a decent car but its sales alone could not make up for the lethargy of Chrysler UK's other offerings.

With no other new cars on the horizon, Chrysler UK found its market share withering in the face of competition from home and abroad, with Japanese manufacturers starting to make their presence felt in Europe. Worse still, the 1970s was an economic cesspool, with inflation in the UK hitting an annual rate of just shy of 25% in 1975. Add in the effects of war, industrial action, and bad management and the outlook was bleak.

Chrysler UK wasn't the only victim of this strife – BLMC's situation was so dire that the government had to step in and rescue it in 1975. Chrysler seized upon this intervention as a way of easing their own fiscal problems, more or less telling the government that they would have to shut down their UK operations unless they received financial aid. Caught between a rock and a hard place, the government gave Chrysler a grant for the specific purpose of building a new small car at Linwood to replace the ageing and ailing Imp.

It would have made sense for the new car to have front-wheel drive. After all, the necessary drivetrain components were already available. In France. And therein lay a problem – Chrysler could not be seen to use UK taxpayers' money to help secure the jobs of French workers.

The new car would therefore be a cut down Avenger with a hatchback bodyshell. This was both good and bad. Good, in that it meant a large saving in development costs and time; bad, in that it would have rear-wheel drive and thus be less space efficient than rivals from Renault, Fiat, and VW – an important factor in a very competitive market sector.

Development of the new car, the Chrysler Sunbeam, proceeded rapidly, and it was launched in 1977. It looked good and drove well enough, but lost out to its front-wheel drive rivals in terms of space. Moreover, the range lacked an affordable halo model that would help to boost its showroom appeal.

By the time that halo model, the Sunbeam Ti, came along in April 1979, Chrysler Europe was no more, having been purchased – lock, stock, and accumulated debts – by PSA in 1978. The Sunbeam would soon find itself wearing a Talbot badge, but for now it remained ostensibly a Chrysler.

Powered by an uprated version of the 1598cc pushrod engine found in the Sunbeam GLS, the Ti was something of a curate's egg: good in parts.

CHRYSLER / TALBOT SUNBEAM Ti

It certainly looked good, with well-executed side stripes, a large front air dam incorporating driving lights, and a neat rear wing enhancing the Sunbeam's already attractive lines. Alloy wheels with low-profile (for the time) tyres, extra instruments, a model-specific gearknob, and optional tartan seat facings completed the package, although some desirable features, notably a rear parcel shelf and passenger side door mirror, were extra-cost options.

As a driver's car, the Ti was good but not quite a match for the best of its rivals. It gripped and handled well, particularly on dry roads, and its steering was precise. Its ride was, however, below class standards, being crashy on less than smooth surfaces. There was axle tramp too, and the gearchange was vague. The biggest issue, however, was the Ti's weight, a consequence of its outmoded drivetrain. To put it into context, the Ti gave away over 200 pounds to the Golf GTI. And with only 100 bhp on tap (the Golf, in 1.6 form, had 110), the Ti's performance wasn't quite able to live up to its looks.

The Ti soldiered on, receiving minor styling and interior updates but nothing in the way of mechanical enhancements until the plug was pulled on the Linwood factory – and with it the Sunbeam and Avenger – in 1981. With bitter irony, Linwood closed in the year that the Sunbeam enjoyed its finest moment, the Sunbeam Lotus winning the World Rally Championship for the works Talbot team.

Although supplanted as the flagship of the Sunbeam range by the much pricier Sunbeam Lotus, the Ti had enough sales appeal to result in approximately 10,000 being built, many of which were subsequently modified for use as rally cars.

Very few examples of the Ti have survived to the present day, at least as road cars. According to DVLA records, only six remain on UK roads, with a further 83 on SORN. Indeed, you're probably more likely to see a Ti on a rally stage than you are on the road.

* Chrysler also acquired Spanish manufacturer Barreiros, but its main importance lay in the extra production capacity it offered and the access it gave to the (then) protected Spanish market.

MATRA RANCHO

AT A GLANCE

Produced: 1977 to 1983
Number left in UK: 2 on the road, 7 on SORN
Engine: 1442cc, four cylinder in-line, OHV
Power output: 80 bhp
Torque: 87 lb ft
Top speed: 91 mph
0-60 mph : 14.2 seconds

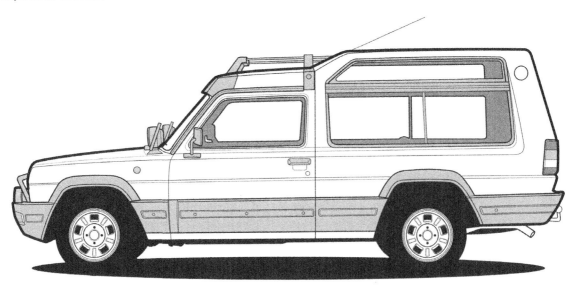

Very few cars can legitimately lay claim to have created a genre. The Matra Rancho can do rather better than that; from humble origins, it became the precursor of not one but two types of car: the soft-roader (or, if you prefer, SUV) and the crossover.

Conceived on a minuscule budget (1.5 million French francs – about £1.6 million), the Rancho was intended by its makers to be a *voiture verte* – a green car. This didn't, however, mean that it was particularly fuel-efficient or long-lasting but simply that it was a car intended to enable people to indulge in some modest off-roading and get that bit closer to nature.

The Rancho's roots lay in the global energy crisis that's mentioned elsewhere in this book. Although Matra Sports survived that particular crisis - largely because its sole product, the Bagheera sports car, was fuel-efficient – it gave Philippe Guédon, the company's technical chief, food for thought. For Guédon, the lack of diversity in Matra's range rendered the company vulnerable to changes in the market. He therefore approached Matra Sports' CEO, Jean-Luc Lagardère, for funding to create a new car.

Lagardère agreed but stipulated that the new car must, above all, be cheap to develop and put into production. With the limited funds available to Guédon, creating an all-new car was out of the question. So he did the next best thing: he took a Simca 1100 pick-up and transformed it into a new type of vehicle: the soft-roader.

The recipe for turning an 1100 into a Rancho included modifying the donor platform, raising the front and rear ride height (to 21cm at the front and 26cm at the rear), adding a beefier grille and bumpers, and fitting matt black wheel-arch extensions and side rubbing strips. The front cabin of the 1100 remained but the bodywork to the rear of it was all new, the difference in height between the two being masked by a black-painted visor and roof rack.

The Rancho's brakes came from the sporty Simca 1100TI, while the Simca 1307/8 (aka the Chrysler Alpine) contributed its 1442cc engine and front seats. The rear seats were raised by 10cm, and a third row of rear-facing seats (which shared their head restraints with the middle row) was available as an option.

The result was a vehicle that looked more like a Range Rover that had been on a Charles Atlas body building course than the offspring of a small light commercial vehicle. Nobody was going to kick sand in a Rancho's, er, grille.

But while the Rancho looked the part, how did it stack up in real life?

Let's start by clearing up a misconception: the Rancho wasn't marketed as a go anywhere, do anything vehicle. Its marketing usually portrayed it as a car that was ideal for aficionados of outdoor pursuits who sought a car with some off-road ability that could carry them and their equipment in comfort whilst also being frugal enough on fuel to use as an everyday car. I say 'usually' because one UK Rancho advert showed it parked outside Harrods, accurately foretelling the era of the 'Chelsea tractor'.

Used within the limitations of its traction and ground clearance, the Rancho was a versatile car. It was pleasant to drive, had reasonably good fuel economy, and could swallow a useful quantity of human and non-human cargoes. Some people even slept in it when camping, their comfort being enhanced somewhat if they had purchased the optional folding bed. If you've ever wondered why the Rancho's rear cabin is higher than the front, it's so that anyone using it as a bed could sit up without bashing their bonce on the underside of the roof.

Although built in right-hand drive form, the Rancho was only ever offered in the UK as a single model. In continental Europe, however, there was a van version (with windows but no rear seats), a convertible (yes, really – the rear bodywork of the Rancho *Découvrable* was covered by a fabric roof with plastic windows), and a plusher model: the Rancho X. There was also a model, the *Grand Raid*, aimed at those who wanted to push their Rancho's off-road limits a little more. This version had a lower-compression engine, enhanced underbody protection, a limited-slip differential, a powered winch, two off road tyres (for the front wheels), and scuttle-mounted spotlights (standard on UK Ranchos) which worked only when the ignition was switched off.

The Rancho gained a new name – Talbot-Matra Rancho – following Peugeot's purchase of Chrysler Europe in 1978 and their decision to revive the Talbot marque. Prior to that, it had been sold as the Matra-Simca Rancho in some markets, the Matra Rancho in the UK, and the Matra-Simca Ranch in Italy.

It never did get four-wheel drive (although Matra tested a rudimentary system that used batteries to drive the rear wheels) nor did it receive much in the way of development. The same 1442cc engine was used throughout its production, and no diesel option was ever offered.

It did, however, manage to earn a mention in a memo to US President Jimmy Carter from his National Security Adviser. It achieved that feat due to Leonid Brezhnev, the leader of the USSR (often wrongly referred to as its President – Mikhail Gorbachev was the only person ever to hold that office), having intimated that the Rancho presented as a gift to him on a state visit to France was the wrong colour. The problem was that Brezhnev had been given a car painted in a colour (green) that he considered to be unlucky. The French officials were quietly informed that a blue Rancho would be more to Brezhnev's liking. Oh, and while they were at it, could they change the colour of the seats as well. The unsuspecting Rancho was hastily taken back to Matra's factory, resprayed blue (a colour the Rancho wasn't actually available in at the time), given a change of seats and re-presented to Brezhnev. The story was carried in many US newspapers in June 1977 and, as mentioned, was reported to US President Carter.

The Rancho was axed in 1983 to make way for Matra's new car: the Renault Espace. It had had a decent innings, with 56,457 being built in its six year production run. And although it wasn't cheap in the UK (£5650 in 1978 as opposed to £4200 for a slightly lower spec model in France), around 6000 were sold here. We didn't know it then but it was the shape of things to come, with SUVs and crossovers dominating much of the present-day market.

Chassis rust, hidden beneath the Rancho's outer skin, has long since accounted for most of them, and pitifully few survive in the UK. According to the DVLA, whose data may be incomplete due to the Rancho's change of marque, just two Ranchos were licensed in the UK as at the third quarter of 2020, with a further seven on SORN. On the bright side, at least one of them is a *Découvrable* that was privately imported.

Chances are, then, that you won't see one on UK roads. Yet in one way they're everywhere: a tiny bit of Rancho DNA can be found every SUV and crossover. That's what it means to be a pioneer.

MAZDA MX-3 1.8 V6

AT A GLANCE

Produced: 1991 to 1997
Number left in UK: 173 on the road, 327 on SORN
Engine: 1845cc, V6, DOHC
Power output: 134 bhp
Torque: 118 lb ft
Top speed: 124 mph
0-60 mph : 8.9 seconds

If the 80s was the decade of the hot hatch, the 90s was most emphatically not. The problem was a simple one: if you owned a hot hatch then you were faced with ever-rising annual insurance premiums if, that is, you could find an insurer willing to accept the risk. For some people, some cars had become quite literally uninsurable.

At the root of this lay an inescapable fact: hot hatchbacks, with their speed, grip, and go-faster styling accoutrements, were a magnet for car thieves. Not the gangs of car thieves that have proliferated in recent years but youngsters who cared little for other people's property and even less for the law. Going for a joyride in a stolen hot hatch became a way of life for some, facilitated by the laughable anti-theft protection offered on cars of that era: a locked hot hatch was easy prey for a car thief with a coat hanger, flathead screwdriver, and about 45 seconds at their disposal. And even if your car wasn't stolen, your radio/cassette almost certainly would be.

That wasn't, of course, the only reason why hot hatchbacks became unpopular with insurers. The other was that they were cars that begged to be driven quickly, with the result that not a few of them ended up either being written off or in need of expensive repairs when their drivers ran out of both talent and road.

That was the scene – in the UK, at least – when the Mazda MX-3 was launched here in 1992. Two flavours were available: 1.6 and 1.8. The 1.6 was powered by a four cylinder engine that developed 88 bhp and was paired with an automatic gearbox. It eventually received a more powerful (108 bhp) engine and became available with a manual 'box, but in no form was it ever remotely as appealing as the range-topping 1.8 litre variant, which not only came with a manual gearbox but also featured what was then the world's smallest V6 production engine. And that's the one we're interested in.

The MX prefix was originally used by Mazda on a series of concept cars that began with the MX-81 of 1981 and included the rotary-engined MX-03 prototype of 1985. In 1989, the MX prefix appeared for the first time on a production car, the MX-5 roadster, and two years later the MX-3 became the second production car to bear the label. However, not all MX-3s were known by that name. Depending on the market, some were sold as the Eunos Presso or the Autozam AZ3 or the Mazda AZ-3.

Unlike many of the cars it competed against, the MX-3 was built on a bespoke platform rather than being based on an existing saloon or hatchback. Its designers used that freedom to give it a waspish-looking coupe body with teardrop headlamps and a large curved glassback. There's a case for saying that it would have benefited from slightly sharper and more aggressive detailing, but the MX-3 was undeniably distinctive as it was. Its interior was, however, rather disappointing: it lacked something of the sparkle of its key rivals, and the quality of the plastics used seemed a little low-rent for a car that wasn't positioned at the budget end of the market. On the other hand, time would show that the MX-3's interior wanted for little in terms of durability.

The MX-3 was not a big car, and Mazda's claims that it was a proper four-seater were somewhat optimistic. Rear seating was made up of a curved, one-piece backrest and two individual seat cushions, and taller people consigned to the rear of an MX-3 would find that both headroom and legroom were in short supply. Its boot was, however, reasonably commodious, and the rear seats folded flat to provide additional cargo capacity.

The jewel in the MX-3's crown was its DOHC, 24 valve, fuel injected V6 engine. Its power output of 134 bhp was respectable albeit both the Renault Clio 16V and VW Golf GTI 16V offered a little more horsepower from engines that had slightly smaller displacements than the Mazda's 1845cc. But with the MX-3 tipping the scales at over 200 kilogrammes more than the 1.9 litre version of the Peugeot 205 GTI, the little V6 engine had its work cut out. It was hardly surprising, therefore, that its acceleration was unexceptional: the MX-3's time of 8.9 seconds for the 0 to 60 mph sprint was bettered by, for example, both the 1.6 and 1.9 litre versions of the 205 GTI as well as the Clio 16V, all of which were markedly less expensive to buy albeit not, perhaps, to insure.

The way in which the V6 delivered its power was not beyond criticism either, being somewhat lacking in urge in the lower reaches of the rev range. On the plus side, it was exceptionally smooth up to and beyond its 7000 rpm red line and delivered a pleasing, if a little too well-suppressed, soundtrack. In a similar manner to the MX-3's styling, its engine was pleasant and distinctive but a bit lacking in excitement.

The same charge could also be laid at the MX-3's road behaviour. It wasn't short of grip and its handling was safe and predictable, with a tendency towards understeer when driven enthusiastically – a consequence of its nose-heavy weight distribution. Not at all bad, but just not quite as sharp as the best hot hatches. On the plus side, its ride quality was very good indeed.

The MX-3's biggest problem lay in its marketing and perception. It wasn't a true alternative to hot hatchbacks; it was just a little too soft at the edges for that. It was, however, an excellent small GT, being a comfortable (in the front anyway),

sure-footed, and civilised car that could be driven long distances without its driver having to be winched out when it reached its destination.

Production of the MX-3 ended in 1998 without a direct replacement being offered by Mazda. According to the DVLA, 173 examples of the V6 version of the MX-3 were taxed for use on UK roads as at the third quarter of 2020, with a further 327 on SORN. Not all of these will be original UK-spec cars, as a number of MX-3s have been privately imported to the UK over the years.

The MX-3 is, truth be told, rather undervalued in the UK. That's a good thing if you want to buy one for a bit of fun, but it doesn't help the model's survival prospects in the longer term. Best enjoy it while you can, then.

PANTHER SOLO 2

AT A GLANCE

Produced: 1990 to 1991
Number left in UK: 1 on the road, 10 on SORN
Engine: 1993cc, four cylinder in-line, turbocharged, DOHC
Power output: 204 bhp
Torque: 200 lb ft
Top speed: 144 mph
0-60 mph : 6.8 seconds

These days Panther (or Panther Westwinds as it was originally known) is remembered mostly for its retro-styled J72, Lima, and Kallista roadsters and its six-wheel roadster prototype, the Panther 6.

But there was a time when the marque produced a mid-engined, all-wheel drive two-seater that at least promised to turn sports car design on its head. That car was the Solo 2.

Now you're probably thinking something like: 'Solo 2? Does that mean there was a Solo 1? And, if so, shouldn't we be told about that too?' And you'd be right to think along those lines because there was indeed a first generation Solo. So let's start at the beginning of the Solo story, shall we?

Panther Westwinds commenced car manufacture in 1972 and over the next few years offered a selection of roadsters that combined olde worlde styling with modern mechanicals. And very nice they were too. Panther also made the Rio, a pricey luxury saloon based on the Triumph Dolomite, the Bugatti Royale–inspired De Ville, which cost £40,000 (more for the drophead version) in 1978. And then there was the 6, a six-wheel (inspired by the Tyrrell P34 F1 car) roadster with an 8.2 litre engine, only one of which

was made before Panther Westwinds went into receivership – a second car was completed later.

Panther emerged from the ashes under Korean ownership. Headed by Young Chul Kim and renamed Panther Car Company, a new model that adhered to the marque's recipe for retro style and modern mechanicals, the Ford V6-powered Kallista roadster, was introduced.

Kim was, however, keen to start building cars that had a more modern vibe. Accordingly, he assembled a team to design an affordable (the target price was £10,000) mid-engined sports car with contemporary styling and well-proven running gear. There was nothing radical about that concept – Fiat had been churning out X1/9s by the truckload for years and Matra had sold a fair number of its three-seat Bagheera sports car – but it promised to open a new market for Panther.

The resulting car was to be called the Panther Solo. It featured a 1.6 litre fuel injected Ford CVH engine, as fitted to the Escort XR3i, with a chassis designed by Len Bailey, best known for his work on the iconic Ford GT40. And to style the car, the services of Ken Greenley,* a tutor at the Royal College of Art, were called upon. Young hoped to put the Solo into production in 1986 and build 1500 to 2000 of them a year. But then he saw the Toyota MR2...

Having decided that the Solo in its original guise couldn't compete with Toyota's new sports car, which was to cost under $9000 in the USA, Kim decided that the Solo would have to move upmarket. That meant giving it more power, more style, and a higher specification.

As there had been some talk of making a four-wheel drive version of the original Solo, equipping its successor with permanent four-wheel drive was a logical decision. It was not, however, simply a case of bolting new running gear to the original Solo chassis. Greenley re-worked his original design, retaining its cab-forward styling, and Bailey's original chassis design was heavily modified.

The Solo 2 might have looked like a roadgoing Group C car but its bodyshell owed more than a little to the aviation industry, being composed of an aluminium honeycomb in a woven glassfibre sandwich, with carbon fibre being used in certain areas. The result was a light, strong, and rigid shell. Compared to the Solo's body, its steering and suspension were positively conventional – the former being an unassisted rack and pinion set up, and the latter featuring MacPherson struts at the front and double wishbones at the rear. Anti-roll bars were not fitted.

In 1987, the Solo 2 was shown at the Frankfurt Motor Show, and a running prototype was tested by *Car* magazine. Production was scheduled to commence the following year, with sales thereafter expected to reach 600 units a year.

That isn't quite how things turned out. The Solo 2 didn't reach the market until 1990, at which time it carried a price tag of £39,950 – £12,000 more than Panther's 1987 estimate, £3000 more than a Lotus Esprit Turbo and £10,000 more than an Renault/Alpine GTA V6 Turbo. And just for good measure, a Lancia Delta integrale could be yours for a fiver under £21,000.

Great things were expected from the Solo 2, and indeed there were a number of things to like about it. For starters, it was the only production car in the world to have a mid-mounted engine and four-wheel drive. Moreover, its drag coefficent of 0.33 was excellent for a mid-engined car – only the Talbot-Matra Murena was slipperier.

And there was more: at high speed, the Solo 2 generated positive downforce front and rear, and its use of composite materials was groundbreaking. It had grip in abundance in both the wet and the dry, and its chassis was exquisitely well balanced. But there was a problem.

Scratch that. There were a few problems. The first was its weight – at 1340 kilogrammes (2950 pounds), it was 250 kilogrammes heavier than Panther's original projections. That might not have mattered so much if the Solo 2 had been blessed with more power than the 204 bhp offered by its turbocharged 2.0 litre Ford engine, but its performance was eclipsed by that of its rivals, many of which were appreciably less expensive, and it didn't help either that the Ford engine suffered from turbo lag and was coarse when extended.

Its unorthodox looks also drew criticism from some quarters. That was harsh, as whilst the Solo 2 was no Ferrari 288 GTO in the aesthetic department, it dared to offer a different, forward-looking take on sports car design. The Solo 2's lack of a boot and limited interior storage space (negligible in cars fitted with the optional – and pointless – rear seats) severely reduced its practicality, but praise was, however, heaped on its first-rate ergonomics and clarity of design.

Still, it was unique. And that in itself should have been a major selling point. But it wasn't. Panther had once hoped to sell 600 Solo 2s a year, but in the end only somewhere between 14 and 21 of them were built. Production ended in 1991 and Panther thereafter closed its doors.

The number of Solo 2s on UK roads varies according to the season. In recent years, however, that number has never exceeded four. The most recent figures available state that 11 Solo 2's are currently known to the DVLA, only one of which was on the road.

Spotting a Panther Solo on the road is no easy task, then. But if you should encounter what appears to be a Group C car on a highway or byway, you'll know exactly what it is... and how lucky you've been to see it.

* Greenley's colleague John Heffernan was also involved in the Solo and Solo 2 projects, but Greenley was principally responsible for the design of both cars.

AC 3000ME

AT A GLANCE
Produced: 1978 to 1985
Number left in UK: 84
Engine: 2994cc, V6, OHV
Power output: 138 bhp
Torque: 173 lb ft
Top speed: 120 mph
0-60 mph : 8.5 seconds

The AC 3000ME began life as a one-off prototype created by Peter Bohanna, an industrial designer, and Robin Stables, a development engineer. Having met whilst working at Lola Cars, the two embarked upon an ambitious project: they would design and build a sports car from the ground up.

The resulting car, the Bohanna-Stables Diablo, was an attractive two seat coupé with a mid-mounted BLMC E-series engine mated to a five-speed gearbox, both acquired from an Austin Maxi development car that had been consigned to a scrapyard, and had an impressive specification that included all round independent suspension and disc brakes, rack and pinion steering, and simple but clever pop-up headlamps.

Bohanna and Stables showed the car at the 1973 Racing Car Show at Olympia in London with the intention of putting it into production themselves. However, it caught the attention of Keith Judd of AC Cars, and both the car and its designers were soon ensconced at AC's Thames Ditton premises.

AC initially contemplated using the 1750cc version of the E-series to power the production version of the Diablo but BLMC declined to supply engines. A Ford engine was therefore chosen, the 3.0 litre V6 Essex unit. This was paired with a 5-speed gearbox of AC's own design in a Hewland casing. The engine wasn't the only part of the Diablo that was changed for production. Indeed, by the time that AC had finished with the Diablo, only its basic shape remained.

AC showed a non-running prototype at the 1973 British Motor Show. It attracted much interest, not least because AC said that it would go into production in 1974 and have a price tag of between £3400 and £3800.

Alas, that isn't what happened. Instead, the 3000ME was the victim of a series of unfortunate events, the first of which was the global energy crisis that followed the 1973 Yom Kippur War, with disastrous effects on the market for powerful, thirsty cars.

Further calamity struck when a prototype 3000ME narrowly failed the steering wheel movement test required under the Type Approval Regulations. The front part of the 3000ME's chassis was redesigned and the ME duly passed the test with ease. Valuable time and money had, however, been lost.

That was bad, but worse soon followed. AC had long been one of the leading manufacturers of the three-wheeled cars that the UK government supplied to people with impaired mobility, and had increasingly come to rely on the revenue thus generated. That income stream was lost when, in 1976, the government decided to replace the three-wheelers with a new state benefit. For AC, it was a hammer blow.

By the time the 3000ME was finally launched at the 1978 British Motor Show, the effect of inflation and development costs meant that the 3000ME went on sale at three times the price originally envisaged. Moreover, it now faced tough competition from the Lotus Esprit, Lancia Montecarlo, and Porsche 924, none of which had existed in 1973. Deliveries started in 1979, but sales were pitifully slow.

When the motoring press finally got their hands on the 3000ME, they liked its looks, its build quality, and the way it felt and sounded like a smaller-engined, more comfortable Ford GT40. On the negative side, its performance was unexceptional and it lacked rear grip. Derek Hurlock, AC's Managing Director, retorted that the ME handled perfectly well, any handling issues being due to motoring journalists' lack of driving skill!

AC never did address the ME's handling issues, but Silverstone-based Rooster Turbos, who also offered a turbo conversion for the ME, found that a slight change to its rear suspension geometry worked wonders.

Its makers had originally planned to build 20 MEs a week, but annual sales barely exceeded that number. Short of revenue, AC began to contract.

Its iconic High Street works in Thames Ditton was sold and operations were shifted to new premises on the edge of town.

Hopes that the ME might yet have its day in the sun revived in 1981, when Ghia mated a 3000ME chassis to a spectacular new body. The resulting AC-Ghia 3000ME was the star of the 1981 Geneva Motor Show, and for a brief time it seemed that Ford might put it into production. Alas, their interest came to nothing. Around the same time, two American businessmen acquired the rights to sell the 3000ME in the USA. They imported a 3000ME minus running gear to the USA, lightly modified the styling, and, with the aid of Carroll Shelby, equipped it with a four-cylinder turbocharged Chrysler engine. They hoped to persuade Chrysler to back the project, but producing a mid-engined sports car did not fit in with the company's plans.

In 1984, a new company, A C (Scotland) PLC, acquired the right to build and sell the 3000ME under licence, and production was shifted to Hillington on the outskirts of Glasgow. Its new makers had great plans for the ME, including the creation of a mark 2 version powered by the 2.5 litre Alfa Romeo *Busso* V6. Moreover, the new company included some gifted and experienced personnel in its ranks, including Brian Spicer (whose CV included a spell as Jensen Motors' chief engineer) and Aubrey Woods, who had worked with both Matra and BRM. With more money, the project might have succeeded, but instead it lasted a little over a year before A C (Scotland) went into receivership.

That wasn't quite the end of the road for the ME, however, as Aubrey Woods and former Ford development engineer John Parsons led a project to produce a new 3000ME-based car, the Ecosse Signature, in Hertfordshire. Two prototypes were built, one of which was tested by *Performance Car*

in 1988. Powered by a 2.0 litre turbocharged Fiat engine, the Signature wowed the testers with its performance and handling. Yet again, however, a lack of funds was the project's undoing, and this time it really was the end for the 3000ME.

In total, 109 3000MEs, including running prototypes, were built: 79 at Thames Ditton, 30 at Hillington. As the DVLA does not list the 3000ME as a model on its database, it's not possible to state how many examples are still licensed for use on UK roads. However, it is understood that 84 examples remain in the UK, including the Alfa-powered AC 2500ME developed at Hillington and the two Ecosse Signature prototypes. A further 18 examples are known to exist outwith the UK, including the AC-Ghia prototype, the Chrysler-engined car, and a chassis used as the basis of the Lincoln Quicksilver concept car.

You might think that such a rare, attractive, and historically significant car (the last AC to be built at Thames Ditton) would command a high price, but at the time of writing a very presentable 3000ME could be yours for less than the price of a good example of that other Essex V6-powered car, the Ford Capri 3.0. Tempting, isn't it?

PIPER GTT & P2

AT A GLANCE

Produced: 1968 to 1973
Number left in UK: 27
Engine: 1593cc, four cylinder in-line, SOHC
Power output: 88 bhp
Torque: 92 lb ft
Top speed: 118 mph
0-60 mph : 9.2 seconds
(Performance figures for Piper GTT with Ford 1.6 litre 'Pinto' engine)

If you're into cars then you'll probably have heard of Piper, most likely as a designer and manufacturer of camshafts for road and racing cars and of performance exhaust systems. But once upon a time, Piper also made cars.

Their story begins in the mid-1960s at Campbell's Garage in Hayes, Kent, home to a successful engine tuning business. There, a small but talented team led by former racing driver George Henrotte built a handful of open-top sports-racing cars, one of which was purchased by Bobby Bell, perhaps best known as the 'Bell' in long-standing Lotus dealers Bell & Colvill.

As the logo used by Campbell's Garage was an image of a kilted piper, it made sense to use it for the cars sold by the company, and thus was the Piper marque born. Over the next few years, Piper made more racing cars, including a Formula 3 car that used Mallite in its construction and a dramatic-looking, closed cockpit racing car, the Piper GTR, an example of which was entered in the 1969 Le Mans 24 Hours but was not permitted to run after race organisers prematurely withdrew its entry following engine problems in practice.

Piper also started to explore road car production. In 1967, the company showed a striking little two-seat coupé, the Piper GT (designed, like the Piper racers, by Tony Hilder), at the Racing Car Show. Although primarily intended for racing, the GT could also be kitted out for road use. At around this time, Brian Sherwood became involved in the company. Though keen to continue with the production of racing cars (he was a racer himself), he believed that the GT's future lay as a road car.

By this time, the premises at Campbell's Garage had become too small to accommodate both the engine tuning and vehicle manufacture businesses. Accordingly, the two enterprises split, with George Henrotte and engine guru Bob Gayler staying at Campbell's Garage, and vehicle production moving with Brian Sherwood to new premises in Wokingham.

Under Sherwood's stewardship, the original Piper GT was developed into the Ford-powered GTT, the swoopy lines of which were underpinned by a tubular spaceframe chassis. Small, light, and low (like a certain other Ford-engined car, it was a mere 40 inches high), the GTT was available in both fully built and component form, the idea behind the latter being that anyone with a modicum of mechanical ability could complete the GTT at home (which took an estimated 30 to 40 hours) and save a bundle of cash in the process.

The GTT went and handled well but, as befitted its racing car heritage, it lacked a few of the conveniences that drivers of road cars were used to. For example, the seats were not adjustable. So if you needed more (or less) legroom you had to take your GTT to its manufacturers so that the seat position could be tailored according to your needs – just like a racing car. Likewise the heavily curved side windows could not be lowered: if you wanted additional ventilation you had to open the sunroof. And on top of that, it had no fuel gauge! Still, these foibles were a small price to pay for a car as striking as the GTT.

In December 1969, Brian Sherwood tragically lost his life in a car crash. That was the end of Piper Cars Limited, but two of its employees - Bill Atkinson, who had joined the company after impressing Brian Sherwood with improvements he had made to his personal GTT, and Tony Waller, who had been Piper Cars' company secretary –

founded a new company, Emmbrook Engineering Limited, and resumed production of Piper road cars.

In 1971, a revised version of the GTT, known as the P2 (for 'Phase 2'), was launched. The P2 shared the GTT's overall shape but was 6 inches longer and an inch higher than its predecessor. There were plenty of other changes, too, with a bonnet scoop replacing the GTT's 'power bulge', different lights at both ends – the rear now having Triumph Dolomite units rather than the earlier Hillman Imp items, and the single faired-in headlamps of the GTT having been replaced by either twin faired-in light units or pop-up lights. The P2 was a little more practical too. The seats were still fixed in place but the pedals were now adjustable. And to complete the package, the P2 even came with a fuel gauge!

In 1973, production moved from Wokingham to rural Lincolnshire. Few cars were built there, however, before events beyond their control caused Atkinson and Waller to call time on car production.

The first of those events was the replacement of Value Added Tax by Purchase Tax on 2 April

1973, a consequence of the UK's admission to the European Economic Community. The significance of the change was that whilst Purchase Tax had not applied to cars sold in component form ('component' being very liberally interpreted by car manufacturers...), VAT did apply. At a stroke, cars sold in component form lost most of the price advantage they enjoyed over ready-built cars, adversely affecting sales. This was followed several months later by the global energy crisis that followed the Yom Kippur War and led to sharp rises in the cost of petrol in the UK. Unsurprisingly, sales of performance cars took something of a nosedive. Even the likes of BMW wasn't immune to the issues arising from the crisis, with production of the groundbreaking 2002 Turbo being brought to a premature end.

Messrs. Atkinson and Waller were able to ride out the economic storm by diversifying into other fields, using their expertise in working with glassfibre reinforced plastic to good effect. Today, Bill Atkinson still drives a Piper – a car that he sold in 1973, bought back in 1989 as a collection of bits, and subsequently restored to impeccable condition.

The Piper GTT and P2 haven't *become* rare sights on UK roads – they've always been very thin on the ground (or, if you prefer, road). It's believed that around 80 were built, of which 57 are known to have survived. And of that number, at least 27 are currently located in the UK.

They may be rare but they've not all been tucked away in museums or air-conditioned garages. Far from it, in fact – Piper owners seem to be of the 'cars are made to be driven' school, so you might just be lucky enough to see one on the road. But if you don't then you'll be sure to find some at the Silverstone Classic and Classic Motor Show at the NEC in any given year. They're well worth seeking out.

JENSEN GT

AT A GLANCE

Produced: 1975 to 1976
Number left in UK: 33 on the road, 25 on SORN
Engine: 1973cc, four cylinder in-line, DOHC
Power output: 144 bhp
Torque: 134 lb ft
Top speed: 113 mph
0-60 mph : 8.8 seconds

West Bromwich-based Jensen Motors was a hive of activity for much of the 1960s. Aside from introducing the striking Interceptor coupé and its four-wheel drive sibling, the innovative FF, the company assembled the Volvo P1800 (until 1963) and Sunbeam Tiger as well as manufacturing the bodyshells for the Austin-Healey 3000.

By 1968, however, production of both the Sunbeam Tiger and the Austin-Healey 3000 had ended, leaving Jensen with production capacity that its current models – the Interceptor and FF – stood no chance of being able to fill. The company's solution to this was to introduce a new Jensen model, one that would be appreciably cheaper than the Interceptor and FF and should sell in significantly higher numbers.

In 1970, Kjell Qvale (pronounced 'Shell Koovalih', lest you be wondering), a Norwegian-American who had made his fortune by importing and selling British and other overseas-made sports and prestige cars in the USA, became the majority shareholder in Jensen.

Under Kvale's stewardship, work which had started the preceding year on a new Jensen roadster gathered impetus. Donald Healey was responsible for the initial design proposals for the roadster, but the task of styling the production car was thereafter handed first to Hugo Poole and subsequently to William Towns.

Getting the styling right was one thing; finding a suitable engine was quite another. Jensen had originally intended to use Vauxhall's new slant-four engine, but this idea was scrapped once it became clear that it would not, in its early form at least, be powerful enough. Discussions were held with BMW, but issues with production volumes and cost meant that the talks failed to bear fruit. Ultimately, Jensen found a willing supplier rather closer to home: Lotus. The Norfolk-based company was developing an advanced four-cylinder engine that seemed to be ideal for use in the new car. A deal was struck with Lotus, and in 1972 the new car, now known as the Jensen-Healey, became the first production car to be equipped with Lotus's 2.0 litre type 907 engine.

On the face of it, there was much to like about the Jensen-Healey. It was an attractive two-seat roadster that combined traditional styling with a technically advanced new engine made by a company noted for the performance of both its road and racing cars.

Unfortunately, the Jensen-Healey was not free of problems, many of which related to the Lotus engine. Qvale had been so eager to get his hands on a suitable engine that he had agreed to buy type 907 units from Lotus without any form of warranty. Jensen might have got away with that if the 907 engine was a proven design that was known to be reliable. But it wasn't, and they didn't. The upshot was that Jensen soon found itself dealing with warranty claims arising from engines with slipping cambelts, oil leaks, and carburettors that were prone to flooding, in addition to claims arising from leaky soft-tops and problems with the Jensen-Healey's paintwork.

Qvale had hoped, somewhat optimistically, to sell 10,000 Jensen-Healeys a year, but this proved to be a pipe dream; in its first year on sale, only 3356 were built.

The situation wasn't helped by the energy crisis that followed the 1973 Yom Kippur War. Fuel prices shot up and sales of gas guzzlers like the Interceptor plummeted. The energy crisis also helped to put paid to Jensen's proposed Interceptor replacement and another planned car,

respectively known internally as the F-type and G-type, but not before the company had spent a considerable amount on development work.

There wasn't much that could be done with the Interceptor, although a coupé version was built in small numbers towards the end of the company's life, but a revised Jensen-Healey was launched in May 1973. This proved to be a much more reliable proposition than its predecessor now that the issues with the Lotus engine had been addressed. However, sales continued to fall well below the volumes the company needed it to achieve.

With Jensen's finances in a spiral dive, Qvale tried one last throw of the dice: a new shooting brake based on the Jensen-Healey would be launched, the Jensen GT. Although the Healey name was missing from the new car (Donald Healey had left Jensen by this time), the 2.0 litre Lotus engine remained, as did the five-speed Getrag gearbox (with dog-leg first) fitted to the latest version of the Jensen-Healey.

The GT, with its 2+2 seating configuration, was 2 inches longer than its roadster sibling and around 100 kilogrammes heavier. It did, however, have a lower drag factor. When tested, the GT was almost able to match the series 2 Jensen-Healey's time of 8.5 seconds for the 0 to 60 mph dash (albeit the gap between the two grew as speed rose) and its top speed of 115 mph.

It shared the same basic suspension design as its older sibling save for spring and damper rates and the addition of a front anti-roll bar (oddly lacking from the Jensen-Healey), the intention being to endow the more expensive and luxurious GT with superior ride quality. Unfortunately, the GT's ride quality deteriorated somewhat on less than smooth road surfaces, and while its grip and handling were acceptable, it had a tendency to wander when exposed to crosswinds. In these respects, it was less accomplished than the Jensen-Healey.

Jensen claimed that the GT was a 2+2, but although it had proper rear seats it was lacking in both legroom and headroom in the rear. On the other hand, the rear seat folded down and gave the GT a useful amount of cargo space. Standard levels of equipment were good and, ride apart, the GT was a more luxurious and refined car than the Jensen-Healey. But at

a launch price of over £4500 in 1975 (£1200 more than a Jensen-Healey), it had to be.

The GT was barely on the market when Jensen went into receivership. It was hoped that the addition of this new model to the Jensen range might help to attract a buyer for the beleaguered company, but it was not to be: Jensen Motors closed its doors in May 1976.

A total of 509 GTs were built during its short production life, many of which ended up in the USA, Jensen's principal market. With more time and more development, it might have become the desirable small shooting brake that Jensen intended it to be. But as the last of the original Jensens (the marque has been revived at least twice), its place in history is assured.

As of the third quarter of 2019, 58 Jensen GTs are known to the DVLA. Of that number, 33 were licensed and the remaining 25 were on SORN. And, in contrast to many other cars, the number of GTs on UK roads is actually increasing, having more than doubled since the corresponding period in 2015.

So while your chances of seeing one remain slim, they are improving.

SUZUKI CAPPUCCINO

AT A GLANCE

Produced: 1991 to 1998
Number left in UK: 190 on the road, 462 on SORN
Engine: 657cc, three cylinder in-line, turbocharged, DOHC
Power output: 63 bhp
Torque: 63 lb ft
Top speed: 83 mph (with limiter connected)
0-60 mph : 11.3 seconds

While many Japanese cars have enjoyed great success in the United Kingdom since large-scale imports started in the 1970s, a very popular class of cars in Japan – the kei class – has failed to make much of an impact here.

Kei class cars (kei being an abbreviation of *keijodōsha*, meaning small car) were introduced in their home market in 1949, their original purpose being to offer a cheap form of four-wheeled transport to people unable to afford full-sized cars. To keep the cost down, kei cars were limited not only in size but also in engine capacity, which was originally restricted to 150cc (for those with four-stroke engines) and 100cc (for those with two-stroke units). The limits on vehicular size and engine capacity were gradually increased over time, and a power limit was introduced after manufacturers started to offer kei cars with turbocharged engines. As of 2021, the maximum length, width, and height are respectively set at 3.4 metres, 1.48 metres, and 2.0 metres; engine capacity is limited to 660cc and engine power to 63 bhp.

Kei cars also benefited from lower rates of purchase tax, road tax, and cheaper insurance premiums. And whilst their small size and

manoeuvrability has made them perfectly suited to Japan's crowed cities, they are also hugely popular in rural areas where they are exempt from the legislation requiring car owners to certify that they have adequate parking for their car(s).

Innovation and ingenuity are hallmarks of kei class vehicle design, with saloons, hatchbacks, coupés, roadsters, vans, and cab-over trucks all having been manufactured to kei class specifications. Futhermore, features such as gull-wing doors, four-wheel drive, and air-conditioning have all appeared on kei class cars.

Few sports cars are built to kei class specifications, but there was a time in the early 1990s when Honda, Autozam (Mazda), and Suzuki all built interesting and attractive kei class sportsters. Sadly, neither the Honda Beat (a pretty, two-seat roadster) nor the gull-winged Autozam AZ-1 coupé were ever officially imported to the UK, although some reached these shores as personal imports. However, the third member of the trio, the Suzuki Cappuccino, was sold in the UK between 1993 and 1995.

First shown at the 1989 Tokyo Motor Show, the Cappuccino was a cute two-seat roadster with a detachable hard top rather than a conventional fabric roof. Being a kei car, it was small - 3.3 metres long, 1.4 metres wide, and 1.2 metres tall – and light, with a kerb weight of just under 680 kilogrammes.

But if the Cappuccino's dimensions were tiny, its specification was anything but. It was powered by a DOHC fuel injected, turbocharged three-cylinder petrol with four valves per cylinder, which drove the rear wheels via a five-speed manual gearbox.

A limited-slip differential was fitted as standard on UK models, and its rack and pinion steering had power assistance. The Cappuccino's suspension set up didn't disappoint either, with double wishbones at the front and upper wishbones with a lower multi-link arrangement at the rear. Braking was by discs all round, with the front discs being ventilated. UK-spec Cappuccinos were not, however, equipped with ABS.

That would be an impressive enough specification for a car from the early 1990s, but Suzuki didn't stop there. Other goodies on UK-spec Cappuccinos included alloy wheels, electric windows, air conditioning, and a steering column that adjusted for both reach and rake. And then there was the roof. Instead of a folding fabric roof, the Cappuccino came with a four-piece aluminium roof with a glass rear window. This offered a choice of four configurations: hard top, targa top with T-bar, targa without T-bar, and fully open roadster. The roof panels were easy to remove and fitted neatly (in the supplied bags) into the Cappuccino's boot. The rear window wasn't removable; instead, it was stowed by manually retracting it into a compartment behind the seats.

Performance was bright rather than exceptional, with the Cappuccino taking 11.3 seconds to reach 60 mph from rest and, like all kei cars of the time, being limited to a top speed of 83 mph. The speed limiter could be disconnected, thereby increasing top speed to 110 mph, but doing so invalidated the manufacturer's warranty. Fuel economy was, as you'd expect from a car as light as the Cappuccino, very good. Its handling was, however, even better than its fuel consumption, thanks to its excellent suspension set up, limited-slip differential, and 50/50 weight distribution. Contemporary reports reckoned it to be at least a match for an MX-5 on a twisty circuit. Its ride was, however, less impressive, with a tendency to become crashy on anything other than billiard-table smooth surfaces.

Suzuki worked wonders to fit as much into such a small package but it's inevitable that something had to give, and that thing was space. The Cappuccino's cabin was attractively designed but was both narrow and lacking in legroom. The boot barely existed in more than name only and became useless when the roof panels were in residence.

It's less of a factor now, but the other main issue with the Cappuccino when new was its price. Kei cars did not benefit from tax breaks in the UK, which meant that Suzuki's diminutive roadster came with a full-sized price tag. At £11,995 in 1994, it was still considerably less than a new Mazda MX-5 but was more expensive than the faster and more versatile warm hatchbacks from Ford, Citroën, Renault, and Vauxhall. Still, if you wanted a brand new roadster, could live with the Cappuccino's lack of space, and didn't want to pay the extra £4500 for an MX-5, then the little Suzuki made perfect sense.

Suzuki imported just over 1100 Cappuccinos to the UK. More would have come but for Suzuki's decision to introduce a slightly updated Cappuccino with a revised engine. This came after the European Union announced that new emissions regulations would be coming into force. As the Cappuccino wasn't a big seller in Europe, Suzuki decided that it was not worth bearing the cost of modifying the engine to meet the new standards. Accordingly, it was withdrawn from sale in the UK in 1995. Production ended in Japan in 1998 after just over 28,000 had been built. It was not replaced in the Suzuki model range.

In the UK, the Cappuccino always made more sense as a fun car to be enjoyed on high days and holidays rather than as a daily driver. This may, in part, explain why its survival rate is relatively high. Of the 1110 Cappuccinos officially sold in the UK (to which should be added a small number of personal imports), 190 were taxed for use in the UK as at the third quarter of 2020, with an additional 462 examples on SORN.

But if you think that the Cappuccino is rare, just trying spotting an Autozam AZ-1 on a UK road...

RENAULT AVANTIME

AT A GLANCE

Produced: 2001 to 2003
Number left in UK: 159 on the road, 144 on SORN
Engine: 2946cc, V6, DOHC
Power output: 207 bhp
Torque: 210 lb ft
Top speed: 128 mph
0-60 mph : 8.8 seconds
(Performance figures for Avantime 3.0 Privilège Automatic)

For thirty-eight years, first Matra Sports and later Matra Automobile built interesting and often innovative cars in and around the small French town of Romorantin, not far from the great châteaux of the Loire.

Matra's first love was the sports car, and for 18 years they turned out a series of mid-engined coupés, each of which brought something new in terms of design or engineering or production methods. And then there was the Rancho, which is discussed elsewhere in this book.

The last Matra sports car rolled off the production line in the summer of 1983, giving way to the first of the three generations of the Renault Espace that Matra would build in partnership with Renault. Theirs was a successful alliance, but nothing lasts forever, and in 1997 Renault announced that the fourth generation Espace, due in 2002, would be built in Renault's own factories.

Renault did not, however, leave their partner totally high and dry. Instead of the Espace, they agreed with Matra's proposal that they build a new car for Renault, one that would use the same platform as the third generation Espace. It would be a unique fusion of coupé, convertible, and MPV, and, as such, would have to carve out its own niche in the market - a daunting prospect alleviated somewhat by Matra's history of successfully bringing innovative cars to the market.

When the new car, then named Coupéspace, broke cover as a concept car at the Geneva Motor Show in 1999, its futuristic lines, courtesy of Renault's Patrick Le Quément, attracted no small amount of attention. Indeed, it's fair to say that the reaction to its appearance satisfied the hopes of the Coupéspace project's design coordinator, Thierry Métroz, who said that he wanted people walking around it for the first time to be continually astonished by what they saw.

A few months later, it appeared again at a motor show, this time in Frankfurt. It was no longer a concept car but one that was scheduled to go into production the following year. There were a few changes, none significant, from the car shown at Geneva, and it had a new name: Avantime.

There were, however, a few wrinkles to sort out before the Avantime could go on sale. The main problem lay with its doors. As a coupé, it had only two doors: two very large and heavy doors, the largest and (at over 50 kilogrammes each) heaviest ever fitted to a production car. And therein lay a problem: conventional doors would need a large opening arc and would place a significant load on the hinges.

Matra's solution was to use what the PR people called 'double kinematic' doors, which was another way of saying that the Avantime used a double-hinged door mechanism. This enabled the doors to open within an acceptable arc without requiring would-be rear seat occupants to be either yoga masters or contortion artists.

The other main issue was with the roof, which made extensive use of glass and had a large opening section. Keeping the weight of the roof down whilst providing it with sufficient support (the Avantime had no B-pillars) made for a tricky engineering challenge that was solved by using aluminium for the roof pillars.

But while the engineering solutions were effective, getting them right took longer than anticipated. The result was that the Avantime didn't appear until late 2001, a year later than scheduled.

And when it did hit the market, its sales fell far below its makers' expectations. Renault and Matra must have hoped that it would repeat the Espace's feat of selling in droves after a poor start (just nine Espaces were sold in its first month on sale), but it was a forlorn hope. A target production figure of 20,000 per annum (far less than the Espace) had been mooted, but only just over 5000 Avantimes were built in the only full calendar year in which it was built. It didn't help that Renault introduced another upmarket avant-garde car in 2001, the Vel Satis. Although the Avantime was the more stylish of the two, the Vel Satis outsold it in a 7:2 ratio.

The situation for both Matra Automobile and the Avantime became critical towards the end of 2002. Matra Automobile's parent company had been seeking a buyer for it since 2000, but there were no takers. Talks had been held with MG Rover with a view to Matra building a revised, re-engineered version of the third generation Espace (to which Matra held the rights) using Rover mechanical components. Unfortunately, the talks failed when the two companies were unable to reach an agreement over production numbers.

With Avantime orders remaining low – circa 15 per day in December 2002 – Matra's parent company wielded the axe: Matra would cease to produce cars and its factories would close in March 2003. There would be no reprieve for car or company.

There are some who think that Matra Automobile could – and should – have been saved. Indeed, Philippe Guédon, a key member of Matra's automotive arm from 1965 until its demise (when he was CEO), has stated that people within Renault felt that the Avantime could have been a success. It just needed more time.

And that begs the question: why wasn't the Avantime a commercial success?

Conventional wisdom has it that it tried to be too many things – coupé, cabriolet, and MPV – without making a decent fist at being any of them. It was pleasant to drive, sure, but it neither went nor handled like a traditional coupé. Being able to open the roof and windows in 'Grand Air' mode was a boon on warm, sunny days but couldn't match the sense of freedom offered by a true convertible. And as for space, the Avantime was strictly a four seater that offered none of the seating or load-carrying flexibility of a true MPV.

But perhaps its critics are missing the point. The Avantime was about its blend of attributes rather than any single one of them. Its looks defied time; it offered ample space for most people and a fair amount of luggage or bric-a-brac; and its ability to go from closed to semi-open made it a comfortable car in which to travel, no matter what the tricks the weather gods might decide to play. Perhaps it was simply just a little too far 'avant' time to catch on.

The Avantime was never a common sight on UK roads. Just under 400 of the 8557 built came to the UK, of which 159 remained on the road as at the third quarter of 2020, with another 144 on SORN. The number of Avantimes on the road has, however, been falling year on year for over a decade. Indeed, over 100 fewer Avantimes are now licensed in the UK compared to the corresponding period in 2015. Chances are, therefore, that it's going to become an even rarer sight than it already is.

LANCIA DELTA HF TURBO

AT A GLANCE
Produced: 1983 to 1992
Number left in UK: 20 on the road, 120 on SORN
Engine: 1585cc, four cylinder in-line, DOHC
Power output: 140 bhp
Torque: 141 lb ft
Top speed: 122 mph
0-60 mph : 7.6 seconds
(Performance figures for Delta HF Turbo i.e.)

Most petrolheads will, if asked to name a sporty version of the Lancia Delta, give a single word reply: *integrale*. A few motorsport lovers might instead suggest the fire-breathing Group B rally version, the Delta S4, and one or two die-hard Lancia fans may, with an eye on distinguishing themselves from the masses, proffer the original *integrale*, the Delta HF 4WD. Chances are, though, that nobody would mention the first of the turbocharged Deltas, the front-wheel drive Delta HF. And that's a pity, for as we shall see it's a fine car that gave nothing away as a driving machine to the best of its rivals in the golden era of the hot hatch.

Although the hot hatch was a creation of the 1970s - Simca having pioneered the concept with its 1100 TI model in 1974 and Volkswagen having redefined it with the Golf GTI in 1976 - it wasn't until the following decade that the concept really caught the imagination of car manufacturers.

It took Lancia until 1982 to enter the arena with the Delta GT, a warmed up version of their attractive mid-sized hatchback.* Launched at the Frankfurt Motor Show in 1979 and offered only as a five-door hatchback, the Delta's boxy but attractive Giugiaro-penned shape was initially home only to

peppy 1.3 and 1.5 litre SOHC engines derived from those used in the Fiat Ritmo (Strada in the UK).

But although the aforementioned Deltas acquired well-deserved reputations as driver's cars, the range-topping 1.5 litre model didn't have the performance to compete with the Golf GTI and its rapidly growing list of rivals. The 100 bhp Delta GT was Lancia's first step on the road to putting that right. However, although it was good to drive, it lacked the pace and showroom appeal necessary to be considered a proper contender for hot hatch honours.

The cavalry was, however, on the way in the shape of the Delta HF. Launched in the summer of 1983, the HF mated the 1.6 litre DOHC engine from the GT to a Garrett T3 turbocharger. And with 130 bhp and 141 lb ft of torque on tap, it had the pace (0 to 60 mph in 7.9 seconds) to match its fine chassis. On the negative side, its power delivery was blighted by turbo lag at lower engine speeds, its power band was relatively narrow and it was fairly thirsty by class standards. Still, as a driving machine it could look any of its rivals squarely in the headlamps. And if you were a fan of rallying, you could order an HF in white with side stripes in the same Martini livery as found on the 037 rally car.

But good as the HF was, the pace of hot hatch development in the mid-1980s meant that it soon found itself up against ever-sterner opposition. In 1985, the Delta HF gained some minor styling enhancements to help distinguish it from lesser Deltas. There was a change of name, too, with the HF now being known as the HF Turbo.

A more significant change came in 1986 to coincide with a mid-life facelift. Sporting a redesigned front end and revised interior, the new Delta HF Turbo i.e. dispensed with the Weber carburettor of preceding HF models and replaced it with fuel injection. In addition, a Garrett T2 turbocharger replaced the T3 unit fitted to earlier HF models. The effect of these changes was a rise in power from 130 bhp to 140 bhp and, more importantly, a significant reduction in turbo lag, thus making the HF Turbo i.e. both faster (0 to 60 mph was now achievable in 7.6 seconds) and more driveable than its predecessors.

Lancia had also taken the opportunity to turn the HF's engine through 180 degrees and cant it 18 degrees forward, thereby lowering the

centre of gravity and enhancing the HF's already excellent handling. They also gave the HF's interior something of a makeover, with notable improvements being made to the dashboard, instrumentation, and trim. The result was the ultimate two-wheel drive Delta: it offered pace, fluid handling, and comfort, and all for £1000 less (in 1986) than the price of a Golf GTI.

But whilst the HF was a serious contender for the hot hatch crown, it was no longer the top performer in the Delta range. It had been supplanted in that role by the mid-engined, four-wheel drive, turbocharged Delta S4 Stradale of 1985. In truth, though, the S4 Stradale shared only its basic shape with other Deltas. Pretty much everything else – from its chassis to its composite bodywork – was bespoke. It was built with a single purpose in mind: to homologate the S4 to compete in Group B motorsport. Lancia was supposed to build 200 roadgoing S4 Stradales to satify the homologation regulations but it's not known whether they in fact did so. What is certain, though, is that an S4 Stradale cost five times as much to buy as a Delta HF Turbo.

The S4 Stradale was followed by another four-wheel drive Delta, the HF 4WD. Unlike the S4, this was a proper Delta with uprated running gear rather than a competition car made to look like its roadgoing cousin. Powered by a turbocharged 2.0 litre engine delivering 165 bhp and 210 lb ft of torque, and with permanent four-wheel drive, the HF 4WD was a seriously quick car by 1980s standards, both in terms of acceleration (60 mph from rest took 6.8 seconds) and cross-country pace.

Homologated for Group A rallying, the HF 4WD swept all before it in the 1987 World Rally Championship. The HF 4WD had, however, a relatively short production life, as in 1987 Lancia introduced an uprated version of it under a new name: the Delta HF integrale. The new model had more power (182 bhp in the first model, eventually rising to 215 in the later Evo 2 version) and its wheel arches were flared so that it could accommodate larger wheels and wider tyres. It would go on to become a veritable legend in both roadgoing and rallying form. The success of the four-wheel drive Deltas meant that the HF Turbo lived in their shadows for the rest of its production life. It remained a highly capable hot hatch but

received little in the way of updates prior to production ending in 1992.

Today, the HF Turbo nestles in the tall grass of semi-obscurity, with only 20 examples licensed for use on UK roads and another 120 on SORN as at the third quarter of 2020. If those figures are accurate (they may refer only to the HF Turbo i.e.), then the HF Turbo is now a rarer car in the UK than the integrale.

There's a flip side to this, however, in that the HF Turbo is much cheaper to buy than an integrale and doesn't have the complexity (and potential expense) of four-wheel drive. It can't come close to matching the integrale's pace, of course, but it's nonetheless a great car to drive. Buy a white one with Martini stripes and you can live the dream without breaking the bank.

* The booted version of the Delta was known as the Prisma. Built between 1982 and 1989, it was aimed at an older target market than the Delta and, consequently, the Prisma range did not include an HF model.

FORD RACING PUMA

AT A GLANCE

Produced: 1999 to 2001
Number left in UK: circa 280
Engine: 1679cc, four cylinder in-line, DOHC
Power output: 153 bhp
Torque: 119 lb ft
Top speed: 121 mph
0-60 mph : 7.4 seconds

I'll admit it: the Ford Puma left me feeling a little cold at first. You can blame the TV commercial for that; there was just no way that I could see the King of Cool wanting to prowl the streets of San Francisco (or anywhere else, for that matter) in a small, Fiesta-based coupé.

I quickly changed my mind about that, for the Puma turned out to be a very special car. Sure, it was a little lacking in horsepower and would have benefited from more aggressive styling, but what it lacked in those departments it more than made up for by the way it drove. Quite simply, it was fun with a capital F.

And then along came a car that addressed the Puma's shortcomings. It carried extra muscle both under the bonnet and on its body. It was quick, sharp, and even more fun than a standard Puma. We know it as the Ford Racing Puma, but it came very close to being launched under its original name: Puma ST160.

The ST160 was revealed at the 1999 Geneva Motor Show. Although initially shown as a concept car, the reality was that Ford planned to put it into limited production. One thousand examples were to be built, with the UK and Germany getting 500

each. But as we shall see, that's not quite what happened.

The ST160 used a tweaked version of the 1.7 litre Zetec SE engine found in standard Pumas. The engine's block and head were unchanged but hotter camshafts, a revised inlet manifold, and a higher performance exhaust system were fitted. This, said Ford, took the power output of the Zetec SE from 125 PS to 160 PS (158 bhp). Other mechanical changes included uprated springs and dampers front and rear, all-round disc brakes (with four-pot Alcon calipers at the front), longer, uprated driveshafts and a viscous limited-slip differential.

In ST160 guise, the Puma's curves grew muscles. There were beefier front and rear wings with heavily flared wheelarches, reworked bumpers, a revised grille and spoiler, attractive 17 inch MIM multi-spoke alloy wheels, and lustrous Imperial Blue paintwork. And those flared wheelarches weren't just for show – aside from having larger wheels, the ST160's front and rear tracks were respectively 7 and 9 centimetres wider than the standard car, giving it a much more dynamic stance. Like the animal whose name it bore, it looked like it was ready to pounce.

The interior of the ST160 was a sea of, what else, blue. The seats (gorgeous Sparco bucket seats for the driver and front seat passenger) were trimmed in blue Alcantara, as were inserts on the door cards and segments of the steering wheel rim. Finally, the pedal rubbers of the standard Puma were replaced by aluminium pedals.

But then something happened on the way to the market. Say goodbye to the ST160 and hello to the Racing Puma, which was the same car. Almost.

So what was different? Well, the Racing Puma (let's call it 'FRP' for short) packed not 158 bhp but 153 bhp, the aluminium pedals were missing, and the limited-slip differential was now a cost option (only 80 or so FRPs were specified with it from new). And there was one other difference: only 500 cars were now scheduled to be built, all right-hand drive versions for the UK market.

To get around homologation regulations, the FRP was technically a standard Puma fitted with the optional Racing Puma pack. When an FRP was ordered, a donor car would be sent from the Puma production line in Germany to Tickford in Bedfordshire for conversion into an FRP. The donor car was supplied without various components and trim items – including seats, bumpers, and alloy wheels – as FRP-spec items would be fitted by Tickford during the conversion process. From the customer perspective, the whole process – from ordering to delivery – could take several months.

That's all good and well, you might say, but what was it like to drive?

The FRP's engine revved happily, aided and abetted by relatively low gear ratios. With a crisp gearchange and satisfyingly rorty exhaust note adding to enjoyment, the FRP felt quick. However, with 153 bhp on tap and a little over a tonne to propel, its performance was good rather than electrifying: the benchmark 0 to 60 mph dash took 7.4 seconds and top speed was 121 mph.

But if the FRP's performance was 'only' good, its road manners were superb. Its turn-in was crisper than a guardsman's salute, its balance was deliciously neutral, and it was blessed with such limpet-like adhesion that it took those wonderful Sparco seats to hold both driver and passenger firmly in place. And, thankfully for a car that could be driven so quickly on winding roads, its brakes did a superb job of bringing it quickly and safely to a halt in both the wet and dry. On the flip side, the FRP was guilty of tramlining on uneven surfaces and its ride quality was decidedly firm.

Ford got the FRP right in all the areas that mattered. Save for one: price. At £23,000 for a new FRP back in 2000, it came in at about £8,000 more than a standard 1.7 litre Puma. Worse still, a Subaru Impreza Turbo, with its 215 bhp engine, four-wheel drive, and the reflected glory of its highly successful rally cousin, cost £2000 less than an FRP. Consequently – and please do stop me if you've heard this one before – Ford struggled to find customers for the FRP.

In the end, Ford ended up supplying 215 FRPs to employees under the company's Management Role Car plan. Three more went to Ford Racing, with rally drivers Colin McRae and Martin Rowe each having the use of one. The rest of the production run went to arm's-length customers.

It's now 20 years since the last FRP left Tickford. In that time, the FRPs value has fallen, stabilised, and risen. And then risen a little more. It hasn't yet become as sought after as, say, a mark 2 RS2000 or a Capri 280 'Brooklands', but it will probably do so in time.

Around 280 FRPs have survived to the present day. Not all of those are roadworthy, but the likelihood is that more and more of them will return to the road as values rise and the cost of repair and restoration (like all Pumas, the FRP isn't exactly immune from corrosion) makes economic sense.

But that's in the future. For now, the FRP remains very much a lesser spotted classic. And a classic it most certainly is. I reckon even the King of Cool himself would agree with me about that.

SUBARU SVX

AT A GLANCE

Produced: 1992 to 1996
Number left in UK: 44 on the road, 103 on SORN
Engine: 3319cc, six cylinder horizontally opposed, DOHC
Power output: 226 bhp
Torque: 228 lb ft
Top speed: 144 mph
0-60 mph : 8.7 seconds

The Avantime isn't the only car in this book that could be launched today and still look like the herald of an era to come; the Subaru SVX shares that distinction and it predates the Renault by nearly a decade.

Launched in 1992, the SVX was, as we shall see, a perplexing marriage of the forward-looking and the idiosyncratic. We'll get to that, but first let's look at its history.

The SVX wasn't Subaru's first crack at building a coupé. That distinction fell to the XT (known as the Alcyone in Japan), a technologically advanced, wedge-shaped 2+2 with individualistic, folded-paper styling - it looked not unlike a third generation Honda Prelude that had been ironed.

Launched in 1985, the XT's specification varied over time and according to market. Common features included air suspension, four-wheel drive on most models (part-time on certain models, permanent on others), a steering wheel with an asymmetric, L-shaped centre, pod-mounted controls for lighting, wipers, and air conditioning, an instrument panel that tilted to match the rake of the (adjustable) steering wheel, 'boxer' engines (1.8 litre four cylinder motors, in both normally aspirated and turbocharged guises, and, later, a 2.7 litre flat-six unit), and either manual or automatic transmission.

In 1.8 litre turbocharged trim, the XT offered fair rather than rapid performance. Handling and grip were reasonable on versions with four-wheel drive but its equilibrium could be upset by the sudden arrival of boost in mid-corner. Like all turbocharged cars of the era, drivers had to learn how to adapt to the engine's power delivery characteristics in order to extract the most out of it.

Its price was also an issue. It was just too expensive when compared to its rivals. It's likely, too, that its technical sophistication and origami styling was as much a blight as a blessing. Accordingly, the XT did not sell in substantial numbers. When production ended in 1991, a whisker under 99,000 had been built, fewer than 10% of which were sold in its home market.

The XT's replacement was first shown as a concept car at the 1989 Tokyo Motor Show. Named SVX (an abbreviated version of 'Subaru Vehicle X'), it was a futuristic-looking coupé from the pen of Giorgietto Giugiaro which eschewed the XT's edgy styling in favour of gentle curves.

Less than three years later, a production version went on sale. It kept the SVX name, albeit it was prefixed with 'Alcyone' in its home market. It was a more upmarket offering than its predecessor and was priced accordingly.

For the £28,000 that UK buyers were asked to pay for an SVX in 1992, they got a car that that was powered by a 3.3 litre, normally aspirated flat-six engine delivering 226 bhp and 228 lb ft of torque, had permanent four-wheel drive (models with front-wheel drive were available in other markets), ventilated brake discs front and rear, an electronic anti-lock braking system, a four-speed automatic gearbox, leather seats with an electrically adjustable driver's seat, air conditioning, and those concept car looks.

The SVX's interior was airy – with all that glass it could be nothing else – but it was strictly a 2+2 rather than a full four-seater. Room in the rear of the SVX was at something of a premium, but it had an ample boot and the rear seats folded flat to provide additional carrying capacity. ts windows were another talking point – only a portion of each of the front and rear windows opened, in a similar manner to the front windows on a De Lorean DMC-12.

The SVX's suspension (McPherson struts at the front, trailing arms at the rear) was much simpler than that of the XT and worked in tandem with its low centre of gravity (courtesy of its boxer engine) and four-wheel drive system to deliver poised handling, good levels of grip, and a compliant ride. Moreover, the SVX's normally aspirated engine meant that power didn't suddenly reach the wheels at inopportune moments. It stopped well too, with its large ventilated discs and ABS system providing strong retardation in both the wet and the dry.

So far, so very groovy. There were, however, a couple of elephants in the SVX's garage. It was heavy, tipping the scales at over 1.6 tonnes. That wouldn't have mattered if it had been endowed with a bit more power, but 226 bhp just wasn't enough to enable it to accelerate as quickly as its rivals. Its top speed was more impressive but owed more to the SVX's excellent aerodynamics (European models boasted a drag factor of 0.285) than an abundance of power. And then there was the gearbox. Subaru didn't have a manual gearbox available that could cope with the 3.3

litre engine's torque, so all SVXs came with a four-speed automatic 'box, to the undoubted chagrin of keen drivers who would have much preferred to do the shifting themselves.

Like its predecessor before it, the SVX struggled to find buyers. Its problem was that it fell between two stools. On one hand, its price made it a direct competitor to offerings from established premium manufacturers like BMW and Audi. And while the SVX compared well in many respects against its prestigious rivals, the premium market sector has always been a hard one to break into. On the other hand, less badge-conscious coupé buyers could pick up a Volkswagen Corrado or Vauxhall Calibra for considerably less than an SVX. And those who fancied a stylish four-wheel drive car could pick up a new Lancia Delta integrale for about £5000 less than the Subaru.

The SVX was a fine car but it's easy to see why it failed to make much of an impact.

All told, 24,379 SVX's were built between 1992 and 1996, just over 10% of which were sold new in Europe. Although available in right-hand drive form, not many came to the UK. According to the DVLA, the number of SVXs on UK roads peaked at just over 230. There are rather fewer today: according to the latest figures from the DVLA, there are 44 SVXs on the road and another 103 on SORN.

At the time of writing, the SVX is rather more affordable now than in its heyday. That's not great news in one sense - low values often lead to cars being scrapped because repairs or restoration don't make economic sense – but on the plus side it means that it is within the reach of anyone looking for an interesting, capable, and, well, different coupé.

RENAULT 16

AT A GLANCE

Produced: 1965 to 1980
Number left in UK: 78 on the road, 21 on SORN
Engine: 1470cc, four cylinder in-line, OHV
Power output: 63 bhp
Torque: 78 lb ft
Top speed: 88 mph
0-60 mph : 16.7 seconds
(Performance figures for the 1.5 litre Renault 16 GL)

Renault struck automotive gold with the Renault 4. Launched in 1961, the R4* took many of its cues from Citroen's successful 2CV: it had front-wheel drive, rack and pinion steering, separate body and chassis units, long-travel suspension to cope with rutted rural roads, and rear seats that lifted out to increase its load-carrying capacity. To this tried, tested, and successful recipe, Renault added a few tweaks of their own: the R4's body was larger and more modern in appearance than the 2CV, it boasted a larger, water-cooled engine giving better performance and it was a hatchback.

Granted, the R4 looked more like a small estate car than the progenitor of the quintessential hatchback shape, but there was no denying its versatility. Unsurprisingly, it sold in great numbers – Renault shifted over a million of them in under five years, and at a time when fewer people could afford to buy cars than today.

The larger models in the Renault range lacked the R4's zest and modernity, however, with the R8, R10, and Dauphine models all featuring traditional saloon styling and rear-mounted engines. They sold well enough, but Renault

boss Pierre Dreyfus was a keen moderniser, both in terms of the company's products and its relationship with its workforce.

Dreyfus had been appointed to the top job at Renault in 1955, and it was under his stewardship that first the Renault 4 and then the Renault 16 went into production. But whereas the R4 could be said to be an intelligent evolution of the concept pioneered by the 2CV, the R16 was a game-changer both for Renault and, indeed, car design in general.

At launch in 1965, the R16's most immediately obvious point of difference from its contemporaries was its shape. Styled in house by Philippe Charbonneaux and Gaston Juchet, and embodying the view espoused by Dreyfus that cars should be viewed as a volume or space rather than just four seats and a boot, the R16's stylish two-box fastback bodyshell set it apart from all other cars in 1965. The same was true of its interior, which placed great importance on style and comfort, as evidenced by its attractive full-width dash, well-padded seats, and generous level of standard equipment.

As for function, Renault had that covered as

well. The R16's cabin offered highly flexible passenger and load-carrying capacity. The rear seat could be moved backwards or forwards, depending on whether more rear legroom or greater cargo space was desired; the back seat could be removed completely or, alternatively, the rear seat squab could be folded forward and the backrest suspended from roof-mounted grab handles; each of the front seats could be reclined so that they and the rear seat squab could be used as a bed; and a combination of a partially suspended rear seat backrest and a partially reclined front seat (or seats) could be used to form what Renault called a 'rally recliner'. Think of a dentist's chair and you'll get the idea.

The first models featured a 1470cc all-aluminium engine that was mounted longitudinally behind the gearbox (a 4-speed manual 'box) and drove the front wheels. Like the R4 and, indeed, the 2CV, the R16's gear lever was mounted on its dashboard, a consequence of the positioning of its gearbox. Its suspension was independent by torsion bars front and rear, these being mounted longitudinally at the front and

transversely at the rear. The result of this was that the R16 had an asymmetric wheelbase, the left side being around 7cm longer than the right.

The R16's dynamic qualities were also favourable, albeit the performance of early versions was the least revolutionary aspect about it. It gripped and handled well, partly due to its weight distribution having benefited from the juxtaposition of its engine and gearbox, and the relatively soft suspension set up that endowed it with plenty of body roll when cornering also ensured that its ride quality was typically French: the R16 cosseted its occupants on rougher road surfaces.

There was nothing else quite like the R16 in 1965. Or 1966. And although the (smaller) front-wheel drive Simca 1100 hatchback came along in 1967, the R16 remained unique in its class until the arrival of the Maxi in 1969. In the meantime, it was named as the European Car of the Year for 1966, a more prestigious accolade then than now, and sold strongly.

Only ever sold in five-door hatchback form (a two-door coupe version made it as far as the prototype stage), the R16 continued into the

1970s, gaining larger, more powerful engines and, on some models, desirable gadgets – including electric front windows, central locking, and headlamp washers – and plush trim.

An automatic version was introduced, as was a five-speed manual gearbox (on the 93 bhp TX model). One thing that it didn't receive, however, was a floor-mounted gearlever – that continued to be dash-mounted right up to the end of production.

That end came in 1980, fifteen years after its launch and five years after its successor, the Renault 20, was introduced. By then, most European manufacturers were making large hatchbacks.

Imports of the R16 to the UK commenced in the year of its launch. It sold steadily in the UK and was once a common sight on our roads. Attrition has taken its toll, however, and now, forty-one years after production ended, fewer than 100 R16s are known to exist in the UK, although numbers have risen a little in the last decade.

Even game-changers have to give best to time.

* Renault concurrently launched the Renault 3, a smaller-engined version of the Renault 4. It ceased production after a year.

CITROËN DYANE

AT A GLANCE

Produced: 1967 to 1983
Number left in UK: 275 on the road, 355 on SORN
Engine: 602cc, two cylinder horizontally opposed, OHV
Power output: 31 bhp
Torque: 30 lb ft
Top speed: 75 mph
0-60 mph : 36.2 seconds
(Power and performance figures for 31 bhp Dyane 6)

To my mind, the Citroën 2CV might just be the greatest car ever made.

Its roots lay in the TPV ('Toute Petit Voiture' – French for 'very small car') project of the 1930s, the intention of which was to produce a simple, rugged, reliable, and versatile car for rural France. Running prototypes with water-cooled engines existed before World War 2, and but for the advent of that conflict it would have been shown at the 1939 Paris Motor Show.

War, invasion, and occupation meant that the TPV project was shelved until the guns once more fell silent. When it finally emerged in production form, as the 2CV, in 1949, it was rugged, simple, and devoid of anything that wasn't essential for it to fulfil its purpose. But its spartan interior and rough edges were the wrapper on a revolution. Now people living in France's rural heartlands could, thanks to its supple, forgiving suspension, take themselves and their wares to market along rough roads and through fields, and at a price that was within their reach rather than their dreams.

The 2CV's small air-cooled engine might have lacked power but it was reliable, easy to work on, and sipped petrol. Its bodywork was also ideally suited to rural life, being easy to remove and replace. Moreover, its full length sunroof meant that it could accommodate items that other cars could not. Little wonder, then, that it sold so well.

It took a long time for a rival to appear. Indeed, it's arguable that a true rival never did. However, Renault did upset its apple cart a little in 1961 with the launch of the Renault 3 and Renault 4. The small Renaults were not as rugged as the 2CV, nor did they need to be: the quality of French rural roads had improved greatly since the 2CV's conception. And with the French economy on the up, people had a little more money in their pockets.

That extra money walked hand in hand with aspiration. For all its qualities, the 2CV was slow, spartan, and somewhat unrefined. And that's where the Renault 4 came in. It shared the space-efficient front-wheel drive layout of the 2CV but married it to a larger, more modern body and more powerful engine. And just to put the cherry on the cake, its hatchback configuration gave it an excellent, highly flexible load carrying ability. Needless to say, it sold like hot cakes.

It took Citroën, by then engaged in other projects

(including the development of rotary-engined technology), several years to respond to the R4. Funds were too tight to cover the development of an all-new model, so Citroën elected to use the existing 2CV platform instead.

Having acquired full control of fellow carmaker Panhard in 1965, Citroën tasked Panhard's design team with the creation of the new car. The design they came up with was essentially a tidied-up, slightly upmarket version of the 2CV with a hatchback and faired-in headlamps.

With a name that paid homage to Panhard's classic Dyna model, the Citroën Dyane was launched in 1967. Its chassis, suspension, and running gear, including its 425cc engine, were all shared with the 2CV. This meant that its performance, with all of 21 bhp on tap, was on the sleepy side of languid. On the other hand, it also inherited the 2CV's supple ride and tenacious roadholding, which made it perfect for rural use. For city drivers, the Dyane could be specified with a centrifugal clutch (known as the Trafficlutch), which significantly reduced the possibility of stalling in heavy traffic.

Although far from the last word in luxury, the Dyane was somewhat less spartan than the (cheaper) 2CV whilst managing to be even more practical. It made the most of its hatchback configuration by having rear seats that could be lifted out as a unit, a flat floor, and (like the 2CV) a folding, full-length sunroof. For sheer practicality, it had few peers.

There was no question, however, that the Dyane needed some extra horsepower. That arrived in 1968, with the launch of the Dyane 4 and Dyane 6. The former had a 435cc engine that developed 26 bhp and the latter initially came with a 28 bhp, 602cc version of the air-cooled twin. Within a few months, the Dyane 6 received a revised version of the 602cc engine, which now offered 31 bhp – a useful increase that took its maximum speed to the far side of 70 mph.

When launched, the Dyane had two windows on each side. In 1970, however, the Dyane's previously solid C-pillars each became home to a window, thus giving it an even more airy interior as well as enhancing its looks. In the same year, the Dyane 4's name was changed: henceforth it would simply be known as the Dyane.

At one time, it was thought that the Dyane

might replace the 2CV. Its production figures comfortably exceeded those of its booted sibling in both 1968 and 1969, but it was the 2CV that proved to be the more popular and enduring model. Dyane production fell below that of the 2CV in 1970 and never again exceeded it.

The Dyane received little in the way of development after 1970. Of the improvements that were made to it, the most significant were the fitment of telescopic dampers in 1975 and front disc brakes in 1977.

Production of the Dyane in France ended in 1982, but continued in Spain and Portugal until the following year. Its van derivative, the Acadiane (launched in 1978, built only in left-hand drive form, and not officially imported to the UK) continued, however, to be built until the summer of 1987. Even so, it too was outlived by the 2CV, production of which finally ceased in 1990.

The old adage about the original being best might not apply to the 2CV and Dyane, but there's no denying that in this case it was the original that was the more popular.

And in terms of UK survival rates, it still is. As at the third quarter of 2020, only 275 Dyanes were licensed in the UK, with a further 355 on SORN. By way of comparison, the equivalent figures for the 2CV were 2832* and 3896.* To put those figures into sharper perspective, 2CV production was, with 3,868,834 built, about 2.5 times that of the Dyane, of which 1,443,583 were produced. In terms of the number of survivors, however, a little over ten times as many 2CVs are still on UK roads as the number of Dyanes.

If you should see a Dyane when out on your travels, don't be tempted to think of it as a poor relation of the 2CV; it is, after all, an even better version of the greatest car ever made...

*Including 26 vans on the road and 12 SORN.

INNOCENTI 90/120

AT A GLANCE

Produced: 1974 to 1982 (with A-series engines)
Number left in UK: unknown, at least two
Engine: 1275cc, four cylinder in-line, OHV
Power output: 64 bhp
Torque: 71 lb ft
Top speed: 90 mph
0-60 mph : 12.6 seconds
(Power and performance figures for Innocenti 120)

All of the cars featured in this book were sold in the UK when new, with one exception: the Innocenti 90/120. So why is it in the book?

Four reasons. One, they were built by a subsidiary of British Leyland Motor Corporation (BLMC); two, they used the same running gear as the Mini; three, a few did make it to the UK; and, four, their story is just too ridiculous to leave out.

That story starts in the 1960s, when Milan-based Innocenti produced and sold BMC and, later, BLMC cars, notably including the Mini, under licence. It was a successful venture that resulted in Innocenti becoming second only to Fiat in terms of the number of cars sold in Italy.

Innocenti was, however, keen to build a car of its own creation. Accordingly, designs for a small hatchback car, provisionally called the Innocenti 750, were commissioned from both Michelotti and Bertone in 1967. Of the two, the sharp, angular, ultra-modern lines of Marcello Gandini's design for Bertone was the clear winner.

Innocenti was keen to proceed with the 750, but the wave of industrial unrest that swept Italy in the so-called 'Hot Autumn' of 1969 took its toll on the company's finances and resulted in the cancellation of the 750 project. However, that wasn't quite the end of it.

In 1972, Innocenti was purchased by BLMC and a young British executive, Geoffrey Robinson, became the new Chairman of Innocenti. Robinson noted that sales of the Innocenti-built Mini had stagnated in the face of competition from the Autobianchi A112, a small hatchback which the Fiat-owned company had introduced in 1969. BLMC and Innocenti had to respond to this threat, and so the decision was taken to dust down Bertone's styling proposal for the 750 and re-work it to accept the Mini's running gear and subframes.

Two years later, the Innocenti 90 and Innocenti 120 (the former used the 998cc A-series engine, the latter employed the larger 1275cc unit) were launched at the Turin Motor Show. They may not have looked like a Mini, what with their sharp lines and modern interiors, but they certainly drove like one. The Mini's fabled steering and handling were present and correct, and while the Innocenti rode no better than a standard Mini its more comfortable seats took the edge off any harshness in the ride quality.

At this juncture, BLMC ought to have been in

a position to offer the Innocenti hatchbacks (less of a mouthful than 'Innocenti 90/120') in the UK as well as in continental Europe. After all, Fiat and Renault, with their respective 127 and 5 models, had already shown that there was a market for small, attractive, front-wheel drive hatchbacks. However, although BLMC did import several Innocenti hatchbacks for evaluation, and company chairman Donald Stokes ran one for a time, they were never officially imported to the UK.

It wasn't that the Innocenti hatchbacks were poor cars. Yes, they had less interior space than a Mini and importing them from Italy would have been an expensive process, but creating a version with a longer wheelbase ought not to have posed too many engineering challenges, and building at least the RHD versions of the Innocenti hatchbacks in the UK would have made financial sense in all but the short term.

The problem, or least one of them, was that BLMC's finances were in a perilous state by late 1974, and the short-term view was therefore of paramount importance. Indeed, BLMC's monetary problems were so grave that only the intervention of the UK government saved it from going out of business in 1975.

Innocenti was meanwhile having its own problems in Italy, due in no small way to BLMC's decision to market a very lightly tweaked version of the Allegro there. Introduced in 1974 and sold as the Innocenti Regent, it made little impact on the Italian market (hardly surprising when it was up against the Alfasud), with just over 11,000 being built in its eighteen-month lifespan. The upshot was that the newly constituted British Leyland (BLMC's successor) decided to end car production in Italy at the end of 1975.

Innocenti and its attractive little hatchback lived to fight another day, however, when the Italian government brokered a deal that saw Alejandro de Tomaso acquire a significant stake in Innocenti in 1976, with BL retaining a 5% share. Production of the 90 and 120 continued and a new, sportier model (the De Tomaso) was introduced. This new model, one of the earliest warm hatches, featured an uprated (71 bhp, later increased to 74 bhp) version of the 1275cc engine, impact-absorbing bumpers and a black air scoop on the bonnet.

Discussions took place between BL and De Tomaso about importing the Innocenti hatchbacks to the UK, but these once more came to naught. A few Innocentis did make their way to the UK as personal imports, and London Garages offered new examples that they had imported from Belgium and converted to right-hand drive, albeit at a price well in excess of what Ford charged for a corresponding Fiesta.

The Innocenti hatchbacks enjoyed long production lives. They were re-engineered in 1982, swapping the Mini components for Daihatsu ones, including the Japanese company's small three cylinder engines in both normally aspirated and turbocharged form. In this guise they continued to be sold until 1993, but never in the United Kingdom.

It's tempting to wonder what might have happened had BLMC/BL taken the plunge and both built and sold the Innocenti hatches in the UK. Had they done so in 1975 or even 1976, they'd have stolen a march on Ford, whose Fiesta hatchback didn't go on sale in the UK until early 1977. Moreover, they'd have had an attractive small hatchback to add to their model range five years before the Metro finally enabled BL to enter that market sector. There's no doubt in my mind that the Innocenti would have sold well in the UK, and I think it's inarguable that it would have restored some sheen to a corporate image tarnished by a succession of below-par new models. As missed opportunities go, it's a doozy.

As the DVLA database doesn't include Innocenti as a separate marque, it's not possible to say how many (or, rather, few) Innocenti hatchbacks there are in the UK. To my certain knowledge, there are at least two currently road legal examples in the UK, and I would expect that there are several more.

Two things are for sure, though: the Innocenti 90 and 120 are rare cars in these parts, and they're very much scarcer than they ought to be.

RENAULT ALPINE GTA V6

AT A GLANCE

Produced: 1984 to 1990
Number left in UK: 20 on the road (GTA V6), 48 on the road (V6 Turbo and Le Mans)
Engine: 2849cc, V6, SOHC
Power output: 158 bhp
Torque: 166 lb ft
Top speed: 139 mph
0-60 mph : 7.5 seconds
(Performance figures for normally aspirated GTA V6)

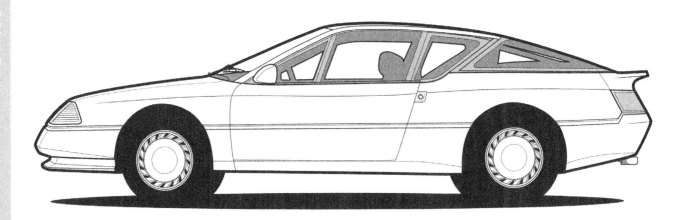

I know what you're thinking: "Hang on, I thought there were 21 cars in this book, not 22."

And you'd be right to think that. There were only 21 cars in this book right up to the point at which it was submitted for publication, which is when I learned that the book, at under 100 pages, was too slim for Amazon to print. Cue the hasty addition of a 22nd car. Call it a bonus. So without further ado, let's get to the car in question: the Renault Alpine GTA V6.

When it arrived in 1984, the GTA had big boots to fill. Alpine's seminal A110 had delighted drivers and won the World Rally Championship, and the A310 that succeeded it offered both flair and, in its later V6 guise, performance.

And fill them it did. The GTA was every inch the modern sports car: its smooth, sleek body cleaved the air so well that its drag factor was a mere 0.28 (the V6 Turbo, with its wider tyres, had a drag factor of 0.30) and its interior looked like it had come from the set of a sci-fi film.

Unlike its predecessors, the GTA was not only sold in the UK but was available in right-hand drive form. But not as an Alpine. That name was already spoken for in the UK, with the Rootes Group having used it on the Sunbeam Alpine roadster in the 1960s, and Chrysler (who acquired Rootes in 1967) having thereafter used it on the UK version of the Simca 1307/8 hatchback. In the UK, therefore, the GTA wore the badge of the company that had owned Alpine since 1973: Renault.

The first GTA to arrive was the normally aspirated version, known simply as the GTA V6, which featured a 2.85 litre version of the well-proven PRV V6 engine. The GTA V6 Turbo followed in 1985. It too used the PRV V6, but in 2.5 litre form. As with the A110 and A310, the GTA's engines were mounted behind the rear axle line, in similar fashion to a Porsche 911 or that other rear-engined, PRV V6-powered car, the DeLorean DMC-12. In terms of power output, both versions of the GTA fell somewhere between the DeLorean and the Porsche, with the V6 delivering a slightly underwhelming 158 bhp and the Turbo a rather more brawny 197 bhp.

The GTA followed in the footsteps of its predecessors by combining a GRP bodyshell with a steel backbone chassis, making it both light and rigid. Its fully independent suspension set-up also paid homage to its competition heritage, with double wishbones and anti-roll bars being fitted front and rear. It wasn't found wanting in the braking department either, with both models having ventilated discs front and rear. Steering was by rack and pinion, with power assistance, which would have added weight and diluted feedback, being neither necessary nor offered.

As the GTA (in V6 Turbo form, at least) was marketed as a more stylish alternative to the Porsche 911, it offered the same 2+2 seating arrangement as the German car. It could carry four people, although those travelling in the back would ideally have been of smaller proportions. Its luggage space wasn't quite so impressive, however, being very limited unless either or both of the rear seats were folded flat to form a stowage area.

Those travelling in the front of a GTA were accommodated in Renault's striking, figure-hugging *Pétale* seats and separated by a centre console that might have been lifted from a certain starship known for making the Kessel run in under 12 parsecs. The driving position was good, and there was ample legroom and headroom in the front. Equipment levels were high, with remote central locking, a fuel computer, and an impressive Philips hi-fi as standard. Buyers who preferred leather to velour or who wanted air conditioning would find both on the options list.

The GTA had a fine specification, then, but how did it go?

In short, very well. The normally aspirated version was reasonably quick, but the Turbo's extra power and torque meant that it could attain over 150 mph and hit 60 mph from rest in around 6.0 seconds; in the mid-1980s, that was enough to consider it a junior supercar. Handling and roadholding were good too, belying the engine's location and rear-heavy weight distribution. The ride was even better, putting many a family car to shame let alone its less supple rivals.

As a package, the GTA V6 Turbo was good enough to trouble both Porsche and Lotus. And for those who loved the GTA's looks but didn't want or need the extra performance of the V6 Turbo, the normally aspirated version was something of a bargain at £5000 less than its blown sibling.

In 1990, a special edition 'Le Mans' model was produced. Based on the GTA V6 Turbo, the Le Mans had revised frontal styling, beefed-up front and rear wheel arches, and three-piece BBS wheels. It also came with a catalytic converter that robbed it of several horsepower, a fate shared by contemporary versions of the GTA V6 and V6 Turbo.

Production of the GTA ended in 1990. Its replacement, the A610, appeared the following year. Although the A610 bore a close visual resemblance to the GTA, none of the body panels were interchangeable between the two. Power was supplied by a turbocharged 3.0 litre version of the trusty V6 (there was no normally aspirated model), power steering was now fitted as standard, and the large faired-in headlamp units of the GTA were replaced by pop-up lights.

The A610 was faster, more stylish, and even more assured than the GTA, but its sales figures were in inverse proportion to its ability – just 818 (of which 67 were right-hand drive versions) were built between 1991 and 1995. By way of comparison, 6473 GTAs were built between 1984 and 1990, with the normally aspirated version accounting for less than a quarter of that total. The problem wasn't with the cars but the badges they wore, particularly in the UK.

Today, just 20 of the normally aspirated GTAs are licensed for use on UK roads. That compares with 48 of the turbocharged versions and 14 A610s. Not a lot for such appealing and accomplished cars.

UK OWNERS' CLUBS

AC Owners' Club	www.acownersclub.co.uk
Avenger Sunbeam Owner's Club	www.asoc.co.uk
BMW Z1 Owners' Group	www.facebook.com/groups/10411983634/
Bug Club	www.bondbugs.co.uk/
Citroën Car Club	www.citroencarclub.org.uk
Innocenti Mini Owners' Club	www.facebook.com/groups/304123226450586/J
Jensen Owners' Club	www.joc.org.uk
Lancia Monte Carlo Consortium	www.lanciamontecarlo.club
Lancia Motor Club	www.lanciamc.co.uk/
Maestro & Montego Owners' Club	www.maestro.org.uk
Matra Enthusiasts' Club UK	www.matra-club.net
Panther Car Club	www.panthercarclub.com
Racing Puma Owners' Club	www.racing-puma.co.uk
Renault Owners' Club	www.renaultownersclub.com
RS Owners' Club	www.rsownersclub.co.uk
Subaru Owners' Club	www.subaruownersclub.com
Suzuki Cappuccino Owners' Register	www.score.org.uk
UK Mazda MX-3 Owners' Club	www.uk-mx3.com

Note: this is not an exhaustive list of clubs that cater for owners and enthusiasts of the cars featured in this book. It is presented for information only and should not be taken as endorsing any or all of the said clubs. Likewise no adverse inference should be drawn from the absence of a club from this list.

ABOUT THE AUTHORS

David M. Milloy (writer)

David practised law for over twenty years before escaping from the legal profession in order to fulfil a childhood ambition by becoming a motoring writer.

Since changing career, David has written for a number of publications in both printed and digital media, including *Classic Car Weekly*, *Complete Kit Car*, *Absolute Lotus*, and *Influx*.

This is David's fourth book. His previous books – *The Ultimate Unofficial F1 Quiz Book*, *The Ultimate Classic Car Quiz Book*, and *The Lost Highway* (a collection of short fictional stories with a supernatural bent) – are all available from Amazon. David is also the co-host, with James Ruppert, of the Bangers and Classics podcast:

www.losthighway.online

Russell Wallis (illustrator)

Russell has been a self employed automotive illustrator and graphic designer for the last 12 years. He has worked with clients on personalised car illustrations designed books for self publishers and much more in between.

He has been interested in cars his whole life, which evolved into a desire to become an automotive designer and illustrator. He spent four years at Coventry University studying automotive design, where he developed his illustrative and graphic design skills.

Russell has a created large portfolio of classic automotive art over the last 12 years, which can be found on his website together with links to his online stores.

www.rjwcreativedesign.co.uk

ALSO BY THE SAME AUTHOR

Paperback:

The Ultimate Unofficial F1 Quiz Book

The Ultimate Classic Car Quiz Book

Kindle Ebook:

The Ultimate Unofficial F1 Quiz Book
(with illustrations by Marcus Ward)

The Lost Highway
(fiction)

Printed in Great Britain
by Amazon